Life Through Death
Discovering the Joy of Repentance

Luke Maguire

Published in 2020 by FeedARead.com Publishing

Copyright © Luke Maguire

The author or authors assert their moral right under the Copyright, Designs and Patents Act, 1988, to be identified as the author or authors of this work.

All Rights reserved. No part of this publication may be reproduced, copied, stored in a retrieval system, or transmitted, in any form or by any means, without the prior written consent of the copyright holder, nor be otherwise circulated in any form of binding or cover other than that in which it is published and without a similar condition being imposed on the subsequent purchaser.

A CIP catalogue record for this title is available from the British Library.

All Scripture quotations are from New Revised Standard Version Bible: Anglicized Edition, copyright © 1989, 1995 National Council of the Churches of Christ in the United States of America. Used by permission. All rights reserved worldwide.

With heartfelt thanks to the people of All Saints Church, Stretford, for bearing with me in love, and to my wife Laura who helps to untangle my grammar.

Contents:

Introduction: An Unexpected Joy	**5**
Chapter 1: The Death and Resurrection of Christ	**13**
Chapter 2: The Call to Repentance	**28**
Chapter 3: Saved by Grace Through Faith	**43**
Chapter 4: United to Christ	**54**
Chapter 5: Saved for Good Works	**66**
Chapter 6: Obedience to Christ	**75**
Chapter 7: The Necessity of Confession	**80**
Chapter 8: Tending the Field of the Heart	**93**
Chapter 9: Attending to our Minds	**108**
Chapter 10: Spiritual Disciplines	**119**
Chapter 11: Attitudes Towards Others	**129**
Chapter 12: A Heart of Praise	**141**
Chapter 13: A Transformed Life	**152**
Conclusion: Onwards into Joy	**158**

Introduction

An Unexpected Joy

When I mention the name of John the Baptist what do you think of? Personally, my mind conjures up an image of a man with a monstrously bushy beard, probably filled with bits of locust and dripping in honey. I picture John scratching where his hair shirt is irritating his skin and I imagine him being rather smelly and not entirely familiar with the finer points of social etiquette.

John was a man who inhabited the wilderness and according to Jesus did not wear fine clothes or allow himself to be moved by the trends and expectations of the society around him (Luke 7:24-26). Some even accused him of having a demon on account of the austerity of his life (Matthew 11:18). John was a prophet and his message was uncompromisingly simple and unmistakably clear. John preached a *'baptism of repentance for the forgiveness of sins' (Mark 1:4, NRSV).* In Matthew's gospel we even get a summary of his preaching: *'Repent, for the kingdom of heaven has come near' (Matthew 3:2, NRSV).* Now, that is not the kind of talk to get you invited out to dinner, and those are not the kind of sermons to make you popular down at the pub, and yet the people were drawn to him. Strangely enough, the gospel writers make a point of telling us that this peculiar man with this rather forceful message managed to draw the whole of the Jerusalem and the Judean countryside to him, and that he baptised people in droves (Matthew 3:5-6). God was up to something, and maybe the images we might be tempted to form of a dour man with a rather hard message need some rethinking. In fact, this John baptised so many people that we now even call him 'the Baptist'; and by the power of the Spirit at work in him, many people made confession of their sins and recommitted themselves to a sincere and diligent walk with God.

As I began to rethink my own picture of John, I made a startling discovery. It was not something I had expected but it made perfect sense, and it is this reflection that has given inspiration to this book. The discovery that I made was that this archetype of repentance, who called multitudes to confession of their sins, was a man welling up with gospel joy. Once I came to that realisation then I began to see his joy everywhere. John was living the joy that comes through repentance. As a child I always wondered why John got the pink candle on the wreath in Advent and not Mary, and why we might choose to reflect on the theme of joy on the Sunday often given over to thinking of this preacher of repentance. But now I think I am beginning to understand.

The first time we meet John is when he is still in his mother's womb at about 6 months gestation. Mary has just received the news that she will be the mother of God's messiah and the angel has told her that her cousin Elizabeth, who had been barren, was now pregnant too. Straight away Mary goes to be with Elizabeth and as she approaches, Elizabeth is filled with the Holy Spirit. By the Spirit's enlightening she prophesies, recognising without being told, that God incarnate was beginning to form in Mary's womb. From the first sound of Mary's voice, the unborn John leaps for joy in Elizabeth's tummy. Already, at such a tender stage in his development, John is sensitive to the Lord's presence and the drawing near of Jesus in foetal form fills him with immense delight.

Many years later, when John is all grown up, we continue to see how much he delights in Jesus. As his disciples begin to desert him to follow after Jesus, someone points this out to him. John's response is simple: *'He who has the bride is the bridegroom. The friend of the bridegroom, who stands and hears him, rejoices greatly at the bridegroom's voice. For this reason my joy has been fulfilled. He must increase, but I must decrease' (John 3:29-30, NRSV).* What John is saying is that he only came to make ready the way for Jesus. The people's hearts ultimately belong to Christ, and so, like the best man at a wedding, he is simply happy to see Jesus enter into lasting relationship with the people He has come to save. John's joy flows from the salvation that Christ is working among us. It makes John happy to see others find their life in Jesus. For John, none of this is about him and everything is about this Jesus, the one he rightly recognises as *'the Lamb of God who takes away the sin of the world'* (John 1:29, NRSV).

For John the preaching of repentance is about preparing people to meet with their king, and to meet with Jesus is nothing other than the joy of salvation. John's desire to recede into the background in order that Jesus might be more greatly exalted reflects the deep humility that characterised his life on earth. And precisely because of this humility before God and his penitent heart, John is able to find his ultimate satisfaction in the glory of Christ. When God is our greatest desire, then we shall never be disappointed for only God is unchanging and nothing can separate us from His love. As the Psalmist writes: *'Take delight in the Lord, and he will give you the desires of your heart.'* (Psalm 37:4, NRSV)

A few years ago, I decided to make my annual retreat at an Orthodox monastery. This was my first face to face encounter with Orthodox monasticism and I was really excited. Funnily enough, the monastery was dedicated to St John the Baptist, and what I found there were living embodiments of the kind of joyful repentance I had discovered in their patron saint. The corporate life of prayer at that monastery was centred on the shared practice of the Jesus Prayer. The Jesus prayer is a simple but profound expression of our trust in Jesus to have mercy on sinners and the power of Jesus as God and King to bring about our redemption. It goes something like this: *Lord Jesus Christ, Son of God, have mercy on me, a sinner.* Never in my life had I heard so many 'Lord, have mercies' than I did at the monastery, and the whole life of the monastery was geared towards heartfelt repentance and spiritual struggle. Even with their faded black robes and their long beards, the monks were reminiscent of John the Baptist; and the preaching of their founder St Sophrony and his own spiritual Father St Silouan the Athonite describe the utter necessity of repentance and its power to open up our hearts to amazing depths of communion with God and with one another. This monastery was a school of repentance, or should I say, a university!

What struck me most about the monks and nuns of the monastery was their deep and serious joy. They were not frivolous or whimsical, neither did they indulge in pointless chatter or unnecessary merry-making. But shining in their eyes and radiating from their faces was a peculiar beauty and sense of contentment that was at once both attractive and compelling. These men and women had found something for which it was worth forsaking everything. These men and women were living out Christ's command to relinquish all worldly comforts and securities in order to follow Him. Their vocation is to live in a particularly concentrated way the authentic Christian life, such that the rest of us might behold a vision of the transformation that comes to those who trust in Jesus. Though crazy in the eyes of the world, these monastics, these warriors of repentance, were living at a level of joy that runs far deeper than any sufferings they might have been enduring. I was captivated.

Since then I have continued to reflect on these themes, especially in preparation for my own preaching. I have come to see repentance as a joyful endeavour, precisely because it opens up for us the riches of life in union with God. Indeed, without repentance there can be no union with God, and without that union we will always be less than fully alive, if not altogether spiritually dead.

Perhaps the words of Jesus that raise the most resistance or cause the most confusion among would-be disciples are those that call us to die: *'He called the crowd with his disciples, and said to them, 'If any want to become my followers, let them deny themselves and take up their cross and follow me. For those who want to save their life will lose it, and those who lose their life for my sake, and for the sake of the gospel, will save it.'' (Mark 8:34-35)* The Christian life is a call to die. The life of a believer is nothing short of a participation in the death and resurrection of Jesus, and as surely as there can be no resurrection until there has been a death, so there can be no new creature, no newness of life, until first the old man of the flesh, the old sinful me, has been crucified with Christ. Repentance is part of that process of death and resurrection. Through the death of repentance, we prepare the ground for the coming of Christ into our lives, and by our humble confession we receive the forgiveness that He offers freely to all who would turn to Him.

    This book seeks to explore the mystery of repentance. As a Christian and as a pastor I am concerned to walk in the fulness of the Christian life, to know Jesus and to see others know and love Him, themselves discovering how we have first been known and loved in Jesus. Therefore, my hope for you as you read this book is that you too will be strengthened in your faith, encouraged by the knowledge of Christ's love for you in all of its vast proportions, and through knowledge of that love, be filled with the fulness of God's life. (Ephesians 3:18-19) I am not a biblical scholar, neither am I an academic theologian. What I offer to you now I offer as a preacher and a pastor, praying that God will stir up within you a deeper repentance, such that together we might participate more fully in the life of Christ. I know that there is so much more that could be said than I have written in this book, and I do not claim to be fully proficient in everything that I have written. My prayer for you is that you will fall in love with Jesus again and again, and moved by His love for you, seek Him with all your heart, such that your joy might be complete in Him.

Chapter 1

The Death and Resurrection of Christ

At the very heart of the Christian faith is the person of Jesus Christ, in whom we have access to God the Father, by the power of the Holy Spirit. It is all about God. For the Christian, God is our highest end and our deepest delight. God is the reason we live and He is our hope in death. In Jesus Christ death has been defeated and through his cross joy has come to all the world. To speak of repentance leading to joy is really to speak of finding God, of drawing near to Him, and discovering in His presence the fullness of life for which He came: *'I came that they may have life, and have it abundantly.' (John 10:10, NRSV).* Jesus came, lived, died and rose again so that we might know both Him and the Father, which is nothing short of eternal life (John 17:3). Repentance leads to joy because repentance leads to God. It is the action, the attitude, the mindset by which we return to the one who has first come to us in Jesus Christ. Repentance opens our hearts to the gracious action of God who rescues us from the very power of death and by His resurrection grants us a share in His incorruptible life.

St Paul had once been the enemy of God, hounding and persecuting God's people, even unto death. He was there minding the coats of those who killed St Stephen, whose face was radiant, shining with the light of Christ, beholding the glory of God, even as they stoned him. St Stephen, in both his life and death, entered into the mystery of Christ's own life. As he lived, he was filled with and empowered by the Spirit of God. As he spoke, he was filled with the wisdom of God. As he died, he was filled with the glory of God, praying for his enemies, just as Christ did on the cross. He endured a torturous death with profound faith as he, like the Christ to whom he had been conformed, commended his spirit to God. He knew that to be joined with Jesus in a death like His, would surely enable a participation in a resurrection like His. St Stephen, like countless martyrs after him, lived to the utmost Christ's call to die and in his dying he discovered the baffling paradox at the heart of the gospel that to truly live, we must first learn to lay down our lives for Christ's sake.

St Paul, who had inflicted so much suffering on the Church was himself to die in chains for Christ's sake. In his letters, St Paul speaks of the surpassing value of knowing Christ:

> *More than that, I regard everything as loss because of the surpassing value of knowing Christ Jesus my Lord. For his sake I have*

suffered the loss of all things, and I regard them as rubbish, in order that I may gain Christ and be found in him, not having a righteousness of my own that comes from the law, but one that comes through faith in Christ, the righteousness from God based on faith. I want to know Christ and the power of his resurrection and the sharing of his sufferings by becoming like him in his death, if somehow I may attain the resurrection from the dead. (Philippians 3:8-11, NRSV)

Having tasted and seen the sweetness of Christ and the glory of his goodness, St Paul recognised that he must let nothing get in the way of his attaining God and living the fulness of the life for which Christ died for him. St Paul understood that all worldly loves and fleshly desires paled in comparison to the splendour of God and that even the greatest of achievements in which he might once have boasted before God and men were as good as rubbish compared to Jesus Christ and all that He has done for us. To be fully alive to God, he must learn to be dead to sin and the pleasures and treasures of this world. Nothing less than a wholesale reorientation of the heart is required.

Repentance begins and ends with Jesus Christ and the glory of God. Repentance leads to Christ who is our life, and apart from His saving death and resurrection, made effective in our lives by the presence and power of the Holy Spirit, there can be no hope of us ever attaining to God. God Himself is both the beginning and the end of our faith, and even our repentance, our desire to turn to Him, depends on His grace. We must therefore begin with the foundations, the basics, the centre-point and crown of our faith, namely Christ crucified and Christ triumphant, Christ humbled and Christ exalted, because in His life, death and resurrection we find the true pattern for our own lives. We are called to be like Him, and in the vision of His saving love, we are compelled to press on to lay hold of He who first became like us such that we might live forever with Him (2 Corinthians 5:14).

There used to be a television programme in which the bosses of companies would go undercover and work alongside the lowest paid workers on their books. They would, for a short time, live the lives of those who had the toughest and least-rewarding roles in their companies. The hope was that they would get fresh insights into what it was really like to work in their business and to experience first-hand some of the difficulties faced by their employees. The intention was to become wiser and better leaders. There was also another programme in which millionaires would go and live on poor housing estates and survive on the same basic levels of income given to individuals on state benefits. During their time they would keep their wealth secret and get to know the people and communities of the places where they had set up camp. At the end, their true identity would be revealed and some generous gifts might be given to some worthy causes or individuals. In both cases, the rich and the powerful for a time lay aside their power and comfort for the sake of getting up close to those who struggle.

In Jesus, God does something similar, but infinitely greater. For love of the world that God has made, He sends His only Son to come and dwell among His people. In Jesus, the Son of God lays aside His glory and majesty and is born of a humble virgin, so that He might identify with and enter into the struggles of humanity. In the one person of Jesus, the divinity of God is united completely, without division and without confusion, to our humanity. He is both fully man and fully God. Therefore, Jesus becomes the very place where heaven and earth collide, where God and man are reconciled; and in His very person, humanity is reunited to God and granted eternal access to the Father. Jesus himself says: *"I am the way, and the truth, and the life. No one comes to the Father except through me.' (John 14:6, NRSV)* Jesus is God's answer to the great chasm that our sinful rebellion has opened up between us and God. In His one person, He becomes the bridge across which we are able to escape the death that comes through separation from the Lord and Giver of Life, and make our way into the freedom of His presence.

Our life comes from God and so to turn our backs on Him is to reject life itself. I have a mobile telephone and it has quite a good battery life. I can use if for many days before the battery loses its charge and finally ceases to work. When that happens, I know that to make it work again I need to reconnect it to a power source and to allow it to be filled with that same power. Whilst my phone is dead, it is still a phone but it is not fulfilling its purpose. There is no life in it. Separated from God, we are like my phone. Without God, we work for a while, but slowly the life drains out of us and one day we die and that death is inevitable. Like my phone we are not able to plug ourselves back in, we are not able to deal with the death that awaits us. What we need is someone to come from the outside and to reconnect us to the mains. This is what God does. In Jesus, humanity, which has been drained of life through sin, is reconnected to God, to the 'mains', from whom all true life and power flow. Jesus is the connection point in which we are plugged back into God, and in Him death is overcome.

Through sin death has entered into the world and only God is big enough to overcome that destruction. The remarkable thing is that God should choose to save a people who have wilfully rebelled against Him. St Paul marvels at this and writes, *'God proves his love for us in that while we still were sinners Christ died for us.' (Romans 5:8, NRSV)* Before we ever thought of God, before we ever considered Him, He was at work making a way for our fellowship with Him to be restored. St John puts it like this: *'For God so loved the world that he gave his only Son, so that everyone who believes in him may not perish but may have eternal life.' (John 3:16, NRSV)* The motivating factor behind the coming of Jesus is love. Love for the world that He has made, love for you and love for me, even whilst we were lost in sin. This is a remarkable love.

Even more remarkable is that God, who rules supreme over all things, should humble Himself in this way. On the night before Jesus was to die, He had a meal with his friends. Before the meal it would have been customary for someone to wash the feet of those who had gathered, and being such a disgusting job, it would normally have fallen to a servant, or else to the least in the fellowship. In this instance, no one had offered to do it, no one was willing to take the least place at the smelly feat of his brothers, until Jesus himself got down from the table. As Jesus stepped down from the highest place, He took off His outer robe and tied a towel around His waist. This is a picture of His incarnation, of His taking on our flesh. In Jesus, the eternal and uncreated God lays aside the glory of heaven and wraps Himself in the humble flesh of created men and women. Then, just as He washed away the dirt of his disciples' feet, He reaches into the brokenness of humanity such that He might heal it and wash it clean of every spot and stain of sin. Remember how Jesus touched the unclean, how He embraced the despised, ate with sinners and was unashamed to associate with the socially outcast and undesirable. Here is a God who loves, here is a God who has a heart of compassion for humanity lost and broken by sin and subject to the power of death. Here is a God who is prepared to roll up his sleeves and take the lowest place, such that we might be exalted with Him to the highest place. This is love.

> *Let the same mind be in you that was in Christ Jesus,*
> *who, though he was in the form of God,*
> *did not regard equality with God*
> *as something to be exploited,*
> *but emptied himself,*
> *taking the form of a slave,*
> *being born in human likeness.*
> *And being found in human form,*
> *he humbled himself*
> *and became obedient to the point of death—*
> *even death on a cross.*
> *(Philippians 2:5-8, NRSV)*

Here St Paul speaks of Jesus emptying Himself. The very ministry of Jesus begins with an act of self-giving, of outpouring. This love, this self-emptying, humble love, leads Jesus to the cross, where in obedience to the Father, He enters even into our death, such that through Him we might enter into life.

Jesus' death was not an accident, neither was it the result of a series of unfortunate events. Throughout John's Gospel we get a strong sense that God was in control and that even Judas' betrayal of Jesus was somehow taken up into God's greater plan of salvation. But why should Jesus die? Why should the Father send His Son to the cross? Jesus came to destroy the works of the devil and to overcome the power of death which have held us captive and held us back from entering into the liberty that belongs to God's children. The sin that separates us from God is the same sin that kills us and steals our eternity. On Jesus, God lays the entire weight of the world's sin, every sin that has been or will be committed from Adam right through to the Lord's return, such that all of the demands of the law against sinners like us might be met in Him. Jesus never sinned and was the only one never to deserve death. Therefore, He becomes for us the perfect sacrifice, sufficient to pay the price for every sin, and in Him the whole debt of sin is paid.

In an amazing prophecy spoken by Isaiah, God speaks of the suffering servanthood of Jesus:

> *Surely he has borne our infirmities*
>   *and carried our diseases;*
> *yet we accounted him stricken,*
>   *struck down by God, and afflicted.*

But he was wounded for our transgressions,
   crushed for our iniquities;
upon him was the punishment that made us whole,
   and by his bruises we are healed.
All we like sheep have gone astray;
   we have all turned to our own way,
and the Lord has laid on him
   the iniquity of us all.
(Isaiah 53:4-6, NRSV)

On the cross as Jesus dies, He cries out, *'My God, my God, why have you forsaken me?' (Mark 15:34, NRSV)* In this moment He experiences for Himself the full effects of the separation that our sin creates between us and God and He descends to the very depths of hell for us, to the furthest point possible from God. If eternal life is to know God, then hell is to be separated from Him forever. Experiencing the fullness of that separation, Jesus goes to the furthest place away from God, such that there might be nowhere left in all creation where He has not already been before us, making a way for our return. Jesus plumbs the deepest depths of hell, such that even the vilest of sinners might have the opportunity to repent and return to God. No one escapes the reach of God's saving love.

When God became man in Jesus, He united the whole of our humanity to Himself. Everything that makes us human – mind, will, emotions, flesh, soul, feelings, and more – He also had. The upshot of all this is that the whole of our humanity was taken to the cross with Him, and the whole of our humanity has been assumed into His saving work. This is really good news. It means that there is not a single part of us that is beyond God's saving love and the power of Christ's cross to heal. All the wounds we bear either through our own sin or the sins of others against us can be healed by His blood.

As Jesus dies the curtain in the Temple is torn. This curtain represented the separation of man from God caused by sin. Until then, only the high priest was allowed to enter behind the curtain where God's presence was manifest, but now, the great high priest, Jesus, has dealt with that separation such that all people might enter God's holy presence. The way into God's presence now stands open and we access the holies of holies through His very own flesh.

But being God, the grave could not hold Jesus and death did not have final word. Being the Lord of Life, the light that no darkness can overcome, Jesus conquers death, and by the power of the Holy Spirit He is raised to the glory of God the Father. As surely as Christ conquers the power of sin and death to set His people free, so too does His resurrection open up for those who would follow Him, a way into life everlasting.

On the day of the resurrection, the women go to tend Jesus' body and to anoint Him for the final time. But as they approach Jesus' burial place, there is a mighty earthquake and an angel rolls aside the stone. Instead of finding a lifeless corpse they find an empty tomb, and instead of the stillness of a graveyard they find the air filled with the angel's proclamation: 'He is not here! He is risen!'

In many ways the tomb signifies the state of fallen humanity. So often our lives are confined by fear, grief, and despair, or else our ability to walk in the spacious garden of the Kingdom of God has been inhibited by the paralysis of sin. The result of sin is both physical and spiritual death and the hardening of our hearts such that they become as stone, completely insensitive to the life of the Spirit. With our cold, stony hearts given over to the sleep of sin, what is needed is nothing short of resurrection, a completely new life. In His mercy, the living God sends His Son to die in our place, and in that act of complete identification, God lies down beside us in the tomb of our sin, and by the power of the life at work within Him, unconquerable and insurmountable, He breaks us out, accomplishing for us that which we could never manage ourselves. By sharing in our death, He makes possible our resurrection. By embracing us in our death, he makes possible our restoration, our return to the God in whom we find our true home.

Hundreds of years before Christ, the prophet Ezekiel was sent to the exiled people of God, who through disobedience had been expelled by God from their land and taken captive to Babylon. In a song of hope, Ezekiel delivers God's promise of restoration, and in doing so he describes with beautiful clarity the very work of our salvation. Through Ezekiel God says:

> *A new heart I will give you, and a new spirit I will put within you; and I will remove from your body the heart of stone and give you a heart of flesh. I will put my spirit within you, and make you follow my statutes and be careful to observe my ordinances. (Ezekiel 36:26-27, NRSV)*

On the sixth day of creation, Jesus formed mankind from the dust of the earth, but that first man did not become a living being until God breathed into him the breath of life (Genesis 2:7). On the day of the resurrection, the first day of the new creation, Jesus appeared among his disciples, who had locked themselves away for fear of the Jews (John 20:19-23). They were themselves inhabiting the narrow confines of their fear, cowering in another sort of tomb, when Jesus, with resurrection power, comes alongside them in their darkness and speaks His peace over them. As He speaks, He breathes on them. 'Receive the Holy Spirit', He says. In this deeply symbolic act, Jesus not only imparts His life-giving Spirit, the same power by which He Himself was raised from the dead, but He also inaugurates a new creation. What we see here is the glorious resurrection of the old fallen humanity, put to death on the cross with Jesus and made a new creature, set free to worship God without fear, holy and righteous in his sight (Luke 1:74-75). In effect, Jesus performs divine CPR; He breathes new life into us and then gives us a heart transplant, removing from our hearts of stone and giving us hearts of flesh, hearts that respond once more to the leading of His Spirit.

But more than this, the rolling away of the stone represents a rolling away of all that separates us from God. Jesus' death and resurrection have removed the barrier that has separated us from God, and by His gracious love, He has secured for us a place with Him forever. The blood of Jesus cleanses us of all unrighteousness and with His death all of our sins are nailed to the cross, such that we might share with Jesus in His march of victory. As St Paul writes so beautifully:

> *And when you were dead in trespasses and the uncircumcision of your flesh, God made you alive together with him, when he forgave us all our trespasses, erasing the record that stood against us with its legal demands. He set this aside, nailing it to the cross. He disarmed the rulers and authorities and made a public*

example of them, triumphing over them in it. (Colossians 2:13-15, NRSV)

Dead people cannot save themselves. Nothing short of a miracle is required to raise the dead. Thanks be to God for Jesus Christ, in whom that mighty work has been accomplished.

Chapter 2

The Call to Repentance

There is no way we can enter into the glorious new resurrection life, free from sin and guilt and shame, participating in the very life of God, unless first we die with Christ. Until the old man is put to death there can be no new life. It is for this reason that the invitation of Christ is first of all a call to die.

> *Now after John was arrested, Jesus came to Galilee, proclaiming the good news of God, and saying, 'The time is fulfilled, and the kingdom of God has come near; repent, and believe in the good news.' (Mark 1:14-15, NRSV)*

It might seem strange to modern ears, but Jesus' proclamation of the Good News and the coming of the Kingdom comes with a direct challenge and a precise instruction: repent! In fact, repentance, it seems, is the only appropriate response to the coming of God's rule and reign in Jesus; repentance accompanied by faith.

Once I was on a train travelling from London to Manchester. Just up the aisle from my family was a sharp and delightful little girl, whose mother was consumed by the conversation she was having on her phone. Understandably the little girl was bored and, seeing that we had a baby, decided to come over to take a look. Her mother glanced over and could see that she was in no danger, even appearing a little relieved that someone else was happy to take the child off her hands for a while. The train slowly pulled into the next station, and the little girl looked up to see where we were before returning to our conversation. Then, just as the train began to pull away, the little girl called out to her mother, 'where did you say we were going?' Her mother called back, looking a little puzzled, 'Wilmslow'. The little girl smiled. 'Then Mummy, I think we've missed our stop.' With horror, the woman suddenly lost all interest in her phone conversation and immediately she hung up. Panicked, she came over and asked us what the next stop would be. Learning that it would be Stockport, she immediately began arranging for someone to meet them at the next station. The little girl seemed oblivious to the drama of it all and was happy to have been able to meet our little baby.

The good news for the woman in our story was that she had the sense to trust the words of her little girl and took immediate action. She realised that she was going the wrong way and allowed this revelation to wake her up from her self-absorption, straight away making plans to get her journey back on track. But what if she had dismissed her daughter's observation? What if she had presumed to know better or imagined that a five-year-old girl could not be capable of having a clearer sense of their progress than she had? Perhaps pride or arrogance might have kept her on the train all the way to Piccadilly!

In many ways, this little story is illustrative of the lives of so many of us. It is like we are heading somewhere on a train, but then we get so distracted by the things of this world and so caught up in ourselves, that we forget all about our destination and the purpose of our journey, and, almost without realising it, we miss our stop. Before long, our lives are heading in completely the wrong direction, and the longer we stay on the train the further we travel from our true destination. We might even end up completely lost.

Jesus' first sermon was a wake-up call. 'You are heading the wrong way, you are in danger of missing your stop, you need to get your lives back on track because the kingdom of God has come near and there is a danger you might go right passed it.' Jesus' call is a call to turn around. In one sense, repentance means exactly that: to make a 180-degree turn, to completely change your way of thinking, your mindset, your attitude, and to get right with God. Repentance is the very act of recognising that we have been wandering away from God and then getting on and doing something about it. And, therefore, repentance requires a certain sacrifice, it requires us to sacrifice our ego and to admit our mistake. True repentance cannot come unless we first crucify our pride. But how glad we are when we have done it.

Repentance mattered to Jesus. It is not the preferred topic of many preachers today, probably because it does not always yield the kinds of sermons that leave a congregation feeling all warm and fuzzy inside; and yet it is the basic invitation to begin a genuine walk with Jesus. Without it, there can be no walk with Jesus, and so preaching without ever issuing a call to repentance is no preaching at all. Perhaps the reluctance of some to speak of what seems so old-fashioned has more to do with the harsh judgementalism of preachers from bygone days and the negative effects of the sandwich-board evangelists with their thundering condemnation of any who have the stomach to listen to them. But Jesus, although His call to repentance is emphatic and absolute, manages to preach the need for a changed life and a reorientation of the heart in a way that holds before us the essentially life-affirming and eternity-saving nature of repentance. It is a completely positive vision. Perhaps this is seen most beautifully in those parables from Luke's gospel in which He explores the themes of lostness and the joy of repentance.

The Lost Sheep – Luke 15:1-7

> *Now all the tax-collectors and sinners were coming near to listen to him. And the Pharisees*

> *and the scribes were grumbling and saying, 'This fellow welcomes sinners and eats with them.' (Luke 15:1-2, NRSV)*

Immediately we see a contrast between the harsh judgementalism of the Pharisees and the welcoming compassion of Jesus. At no point in the gospels does Jesus condone sinful living and nowhere does He minimise the utterly destructive effects of sin in a person's life; and yet here He is, mixing with those whose sin has defined their public image. The Pharisees cannot comprehend how any teacher of the people and self-respecting rabbi could be associated with sinners like these. But Jesus' mission was always to identify with the weak, the lost and the broken; and Jesus' whole presence among us was the expression of God's heart to seek out and save the lost. Yes, God hates sin, but God also desires for all to be delivered from its power and to find true life in Him. Jesus looks on the sinner with compassion, and it is this attitude towards those who resist God and His ways that reveals the depths of His love and the nature of His glory. How reassuring this is to us when we fall short of God's glory. How reassuring is the knowledge that those who humbly return to God will not be driven away, regardless of how far they have strayed from Him.

But there is also a warning here. It is precisely those who know their fallenness and who are fully aware of their need for forgiveness and amendment of life that come most easily to Jesus. Whereas the self-satisfied and the proud, those who trust in their own righteousness before God, are imprisoned by their own ego. Hardened by pride, they inadvertently find themselves resisting the workings of God's grace. To those who have built up their own edifice of self-righteousness, the thought of laying it down in order to draw close to God is beyond their reasoning. The very thing in which they trust for their salvation has become the very wall that keeps them from it.

Somehow, Jesus needs to expose their hardness of heart and show both them and us that God's ways are indeed ways of justice and truth, but also ways of compassion and mercy. So, like a good teacher, He tells some stories.

The first story is the story of a shepherd. This shepherd has exactly one hundred sheep and he knows each of them by name. Each one is precious to him and each one is known by him. One night he is checking his flock, making sure that each one has stayed close. Suddenly, he realises with horror that one little sheep is missing. It is getting dark and they are deep in the wilderness. The roads are rough and uneven, even perilous; the thorns and briers are enough to rip through your flesh. Furthermore, the beasts of the night are hungry, looking for unsuspecting victims to devour.

The shepherd is a good shepherd. His whole life has revolved around protecting and nurturing the flock, and he will not stop now. He cannot imagine his flock without that missing sheep and he is determined to find her. So, he sets off into the falling darkness. And as he goes, he too risks the jaws of the wild animals and the danger of falling to his death. Eventually, he hears the faint bleating of a little sheep, and filled with compassion he bashes his way through the thorns and presses on into the shadows until he has recovered the sheep that was lost. His own skin is now covered in blood and his body is weary from the fight, but lovingly he frees the sheep, untangling its wool from the brambles. Then, noticing how the sheep is injured, he takes it upon his shoulders and retraces his steps, once again vulnerable to all the dangers of the night, until finally he has brought the sheep safely home.

What Jesus offers us here is a picture of salvation. The sheep is lost, pitifully lost and unable to rescue itself, unable to make its own way home. Unless the shepherd comes to rescue her, she will die in the wilderness and become food for the vultures. But the shepherd, filled with compassion, enters right into the painful mess of the sheep's lostness and makes a way for the sheep to be rescued. All the sheep must do is cry out to her shepherd and then, when he comes, yield into the shepherd's embrace, and allow herself to be carried home. The sheep must acknowledge her need of salvation and her utter helplessness without the protective embrace of her master.

> *And when he comes home, he calls together his friends and neighbours, saying to them, "Rejoice with me, for I have found my sheep that was lost." Just so, I tell you, there will be more joy in heaven over one sinner who repents than over ninety-nine righteous people who need no repentance. (Luke 15:6-7, NRSV)*

The love with which the shepherd holds the sheep is reflected in the joy he feels over her salvation. So it is with us. God takes no pleasure in the destruction of the wayward but, loving everything that He has made, He goes to the very depths of hell that all might turn to Him and live.

The Lost Coin – Luke 15:8-10

Then Jesus tells the story of a woman who had ten silver coins. She loses one and cannot rest until she has found it. Her search is relentless and diligent, she knows the value of what she has lost and thinks it worth the effort of turning the house upside down to find it. This woman, in her painstaking search, lights a lamp and shines it into every dark corner of her house until she sees that little coin reflecting back the lamplight. Again, this is a picture of God's salvific action, and what joy is the Lord's when a sinner repents, and what joy there is among the angels, who work to see our salvation.

In many ways this story is like the first. In each story both the objects of the search - the sheep and the coin - cannot find themselves. Both of them are lost and completely dependent on the initiative of others. In both cases the value of what is sought makes the search worth the effort, worth the risk. Here Jesus reminds us yet again that we are precious in His sight and that He will leave no dark corner of creation unvisited in His search for the lost. How wonderful it is to know that the living God sees in us a value so great that He would not spare His only Son for the sake of our redemption.

Perhaps one of the most beautiful aspects of God's redemptive work is that the initiative lay entirely with Him. The whole of the New Testament points to the fact that Christ's incarnation, death and resurrection were accomplished before any of us had even thought to love Him. God's grace makes the first move in His reconciliation with the world, and that first move is Jesus.

The Lost Son – Luke 15:11-32

In the third story, we hear of a man who had two sons. The youngest of the two approached his father and asked for his share of the inheritance up front. This is a shocking request since to ask such a thing is tantamount to saying 'I'm more interested in what you have to give me than in the life we share together'. Already, we are tuned into how these stories work, and perhaps we are already beginning to examine our own attitudes towards God and our relationship with Him. I wonder, how often we have been more eager to lay hold of the blessings God gives than we are to lay hold of the one who gives them?

Either way, the son packs up his stuff and leaves home, setting off for new pastures where he is free to squander his share of the inheritance on dissolute living. Soon enough the money runs out and the freedom-seeking son finds himself in the prison of poverty, his financial predicament exacerbated by a famine that has begun to ravage the land. Things could not get any worse. Now he is seeking whatever work he can find, and before long he is tending the pigs of a man who will not even let him share their trough.

In his utter desperation his thoughts turn back to home. He suddenly appreciates what he has thrown away and no longer despises what he might once have felt were the constrictive relationships and routines of the parental home. Now he longs for their comfort and their stability. Freedom, it turns out, is not to be found in the places of self-gratification, because his new life has left him more vulnerable to death than he ever was under his father's care.

But the son has not fully understood the character of his father. He imagines that his return will necessitate much grovelling, and he decides to make his way home in order to offer himself as a slave, never imagining that he might be received as a son. He has underestimated the strength of the father's love, because whilst the profligate son makes his way home, ashamed of his conduct, his father is waiting for him. In fact, his father has not stopped waiting. Every day he has had one eye on the horizon, willing the return of his son, whom he cannot bear to lose. And so, when he sees him coming, he drops everything and runs to meet him. No reproach, no judgement, just the simple delight of a man who has been reunited with his long-lost son.

The son's response is instructive for us: *"Father, I have sinned against heaven and before you; I am no longer worthy to be called your son"* (Luke 15:21, NRSV). Perhaps Jesus has now turned one eye towards His listeners. The son has accepted full responsibility for his actions and has rightfully seen that his sinful living has not only injured his earthly relationships, but has also ruptured his relationship with God, for indeed the two are inseparable. There is no sin that does not simultaneously disrupt our relationships with both God and with others. And indeed, in our own sinfulness, we might also recognise that we have scorned the blessings of sonship, and in our turning away from God, we have rejected His fatherhood.

Yet remarkably, the father's joy at the return of his son eclipses all talk of blame and retribution. The father's dream had simply been to see their relationship restored, and so the son's return becomes the cause for a mighty celebration: *"And get the fatted calf and kill it, and let us eat and celebrate; for this son of mine was dead and is alive again; he was lost and is found!" (Luke 15:23-24, NRSV).* Notice how Jesus uses the image of resurrection. He was dead and is alive again, he was lost and now is found. The return of a sinner to the Father in humble repentance is nothing short of a new birth and the complete renewal of their personhood. When we come to our senses about the sin in our lives and make our way back to the Father, when we make the humble act of confessing and repenting of our sins, then Father God will surely welcome us home as long-lost sons and daughters, not counting our past sins against us.

How far removed is this attitude from the embittered and pharisaic attitudes of the religious professionals with whom Jesus had to contend? What a contrast we see between Jesus' gracious love and the merciless self-righteousness of the Pharisees. In the story, Jesus continues with the return of the older brother from the fields. This brother hears all the commotion and asks about what is happening. But when the servants inform him of his brother's return, he storms up to his father, filled with furious indignation. It is not fair. It is simply not fair. How come his father has lavished so much grace on the son who wasted his inheritance, and yet has never done a fraction as much for him who stayed faithfully at his side? It is a good question, but it misses the nature of grace, because, at heart, grace is deeply unfair by any worldly understanding of the word. Grace is unfair because it involves people getting precisely what they do not deserve, and to the self-righteous and those who trust in their own goodness, such a thought can never be countenanced because it undermines the whole system by which they bolster their own ego.

In today's world it is normal to talk about people getting their 'just desserts'. The media makes a lot of money by exposing sin and then subjecting sinners to public disdain. But if we are honest, who among us is without sin? Who among us would be comfortable if the BBC were to announce that they had a machine that could turn our thoughts into a soap opera, and that our most private and secret thoughts and desires would be aired for the nation to see? The reality is that if our thoughts, words and deeds are to be the measure of our worthiness for relationship with God, then none of us is worthy of salvation. The older brother is right, and the fatted calf should not be killed for us. *'For the wages of sin is death' (Romans 6:23, NRSV).*

But what if we look back to the story of the coin. The coin is worth finding because it has intrinsic value, because it is made of something precious, which is no less precious for being lost. It would be silly to suggest that its monetary value is reduced because it was naughty enough to roll off the table and down beneath the cupboard. The behaviour of the coin, or even the sheep for that matter, do nothing to change their intrinsic worth. They are worth finding because they have value in and of themselves. Our worth in God's eyes is not measured by what we do, but by who we are. Before we are saints or sinners, we are first and foremost human beings made in the image of God. Deeper than all our sin lies God's image, and although we sometimes do a pretty good job of burying it, it is nevertheless there, and our intrinsic value and dignity as human beings, made and loved by God, will never change.

This is precisely why Jesus died on the cross, suffering for the ungodly before anyone ever deserved it. God sees in each of us a value that even we might struggle to see. Sure, we might need new clothes before we can re-enter the family home, just as the prodigal was re-clothed by his father, but Jesus is at work sorting out our wardrobe – He will clothe us with His own righteousness. Sin grieves the Father precisely because it robs Him of His children, and Jesus' work is entirely about restoring what has been lost through our fall into sin. There is no room for pride here and no room for merit, other than the merits of Jesus' death and resurrection. The God of heaven and the cross of Christ can be our only boast (2 Corinthians 10:17) because our salvation is entirely His work. None of us is worthy of salvation because of what we have or have not done, but only because of what God has done for us in Christ. If we insist on people getting their 'just desserts', then we too must expect to eat humble pie!

So, Jesus calls us to repentance, to turn our lives around and to reorient our hearts such that instead of pulling away from Him and against His will, we come to our senses, recognise our waywardness and set about returning home. Like the sheep in Jesus' story, we cry out to the master, and as we are assured in the scriptures, everyone who calls on the name of the Lord will be saved (Acts 2:21). In Jesus, God comes to us and invites us to yield into His strong and gentle hands such that He might carry us back to the Father, to the safety of the fold.

Chapter 3

Saved by Grace through Faith

Perhaps one of the most startling discoveries for anyone new to the Christian faith is the manner in which we lay hold of our salvation. It is quite easy to assume that Christianity is at heart no different from the other world religions, that just like them, salvation is something we earn through good deeds, karma, or through the meticulous keeping of certain rules and regulations. In such a view, it is almost like collecting coupons from a cereal packet, and one day, if we manage to collect enough little cardboard tokens, we are granted admittance to some theme park free of charge. In this sense, heaven is a prize for trying hard, or else payment for fulfilling our duties and obligations. In such a view, faith is a great big rewards system and the eternal destiny of our lives depends on our own works, on our own righteousness, on our own merit. Such a view leaves us with the haunting question: have I done enough?

It is no wonder that this is the prevailing view among religious people around the world, and even among those who are not religious but have a view about how religion should be. It seems incredibly fair;

you get what you deserve and you deserve what you get. But such a view is based on a flawed assumption: namely, that salvation lies within our own power and that humanity contains within itself the resources to make right its wrongs before God. The second problem with this view is that it presupposes a relationship with God that is really quite impersonal and terribly functional, completely failing to recognise that God's primary interest in salvation is restoring friendship with His people and not simply admitting them to a heavenly theme park. God is not Santa Claus and the heart of the life of heaven is His presence and not His presents.

The Christian tradition teaches us that humanity, since the fall, is subject to death and that none of us has managed to live a sinless life. The consequence of this is a brokenness that itself renders us incapable of ascending 'the mountain of faith' towards God by our own effort. It is a predicament that requires God Himself to come down from His 'mountain' such that He might seek us out, renew us and carry us home. This is exactly what we have been exploring; this is what we see enacted at the last supper when Jesus washes His disciples' feet.

Forty days after Jesus' resurrection He gathered His disciples together on the mount of olives and He instructed them to wait in Jerusalem until they had been clothed with power from on high (Luke 24:49). Then, He ascended bodily into the heavens where He took His place eternally at the right hand of the Father. This event is particularly significant because, as the Church affirms, Jesus was raised bodily from the dead. The body of the resurrected Jesus was certainly different from his pre-resurrection body: He could walk through walls and He could appear and disappear, for example. But Jesus also took pains to show His disciples that He was not a ghost or an apparition, or even a purely spiritual being: He ate fish, He cooked breakfast, He encouraged them to touch the wounds on His body. This means that when He ascended, He took the whole of our humanity with Him into heaven: mind, body and soul, everything. This means that because of Jesus' incarnation, death, resurrection and ascension, the whole of our humanity and everything that makes us human is forever united to God and seated with Him at the right hand of the Father. St Paul writes: *'But God, who is rich in mercy, out of the great love with which he loved us even when we were dead through our trespasses, made us alive together with Christ—by grace you have been saved— and raised us up with him and seated us with him in the heavenly places in Christ Jesus, so that in the ages to come he might show the immeasurable riches of his grace in kindness towards us in Christ Jesus.' (Ephesians 2:4-7, NRSV)* The good news here is that God has opened up a way for us to enter directly into His presence, entirely through the works of Christ, something we could never do by our own effort. Whilst we were dead in our sins, God made us alive together with Christ, and by the power of His Spirit, He has enabled us to share in the righteousness of Jesus, by which we are made worthy to stand before God.

Jesus told the story of two men praying in the temple. One was a Pharisee, a man belonging to a sect renowned for their purity of life and their fastidious keeping of all sorts of religious rules and regulations. Filled with pride, the Pharisee begins to pray in a boastful way and he sings his own praises before God. The Pharisee feels confident before God because he is so convinced of his own righteousness and the quality of his own efforts in the faith. After all, he keeps all the rules. He even looks over to those around him and thanks God that he is not a sinner like them. His prayer comes from a strong delusion about the state of his own soul and it stands in marked contrast to the prayer of the second man who happens to be a tax collector. Tax collectors were considered to be both men of sin and traitors of the nation by virtue of being on the payroll of the occupying Roman authorities and occasionally defrauding the people for their own gain. But this tax collector cannot even lift his eyes to heaven. He is filled with a profound sense of his own sinfulness before God, and he simply cries out, asking God to have mercy on his wretched soul. Jesus concludes the story, seeking to expose the proud hypocrisy of those who trust in their own righteousness, and He says of the tax collector, *'I tell you, this man went down to his home justified rather than the other; for all who exalt themselves will be humbled, but all who humble themselves will be exalted.' (Luke 18:14, NRSV)*

The message is clear that it is through humility, through humble contrition and penitence of heart, that we are justified before God and not because of any good works of our own. Justification, that declaration of our righteousness before the judgement seat of God, is something that God does and is given freely to those who are humble enough to acknowledge their need of it. In perhaps one of the central passages on this wonderful truth, St Paul writes to the church in Rome:

> *'…since all have sinned and fall short of the glory of God; they are now justified by his grace as a gift, through the redemption that is in Christ Jesus, whom God put forward as a sacrifice of atonement by his blood, effective through faith. He did this to show his righteousness, because in his divine forbearance he had passed over the sins previously committed; it was to prove at the present time that he himself is righteous and that he justifies the one who has faith in Jesus.' (Romans 3:23-26, NRSV)*

What we discover is that the renewal of our relationship with God and our being made right with Him is entirely His work and comes as a free gift through faith. Our part in salvation is faith; the rest is the work of God Himself. Jesus' death is a sacrifice, a means of fulfilling the requirements of the law, such that by standing in our place and suffering the penalty for our sin, we can be freed from its power and set free to enter into a new and living relationship with God. When Jesus dies, a wonderful exchange takes place; taking our humanity to the cross, He who was sinless takes our sins from us and gives us in return His own incorruptible life.

Therefore, contrary to the preaching of those who speak of salvation as a reward for our own good works, we proclaim instead salvation by the good works of Jesus and the merits of His death and resurrection, received and imparted to us through faith. But what is faith? What does it mean to believe in Jesus for salvation? Quite often when I go into the pub, or stand in a queue at the post office in my dog collar, people begin to make their excuses for not going to church, without me even so much as raising the issue. One of the lines I often hear goes something like this: *'I don't go to church but I believe in God, I know He definitely exists'*. But is a simple belief in the existence of God what the Bible means when it speaks of faith? In the letter of James, we read of how even the demons believe in the existence of God and tremble before Him, but that does not mean that they have faith (James 2:19). In fact, you will not find a theologian on earth or a biblical scholar anywhere that knows the doctrines of scripture and the intricacies of Christian theology as well as the devil, and yet clearly he has not been saved. Therefore, faith must be more than an intellectual acknowledgement of the existence of God. The devil knows better than any of us that Jesus died for our sins and rose again for our redemption, he knows better than any that the blood of Jesus is sufficient to wipe away every spot and stain of sin; that is precisely why he fights so hard against genuine Christian faith. So, if faith is more than simply knowing the truth, what is it?

At this point many preachers have turned to the story of Charles Blondin, the famous Victorian tightrope walker. For those of you who do not know his story, Charles Blondin's greatest feat was to cross Niagara Falls between Canada and the Unites States on a tightrope barely two inches wide, and entirely without a safety net. The first time across was remarkable enough, but over the following days he crossed numerous times, each crossing becoming more daring than the last. One time he took a camera with him; not a small polaroid or digital number, but one of those great big clunky things they used to use about 150 years ago, complete with tripod. Naturally he took a picture half-way across. On subsequent crossings he walked backwards, he crossed with a sack over his head, and perhaps, most daring of all, he carried across another human being.

Imagine that Blondin had asked you to cross with him, to cling to his back as he carried you across that perilous gorge. What would you have said? Would you have done it? You would have just seen him perform all of those amazing stunts and you would have just witnessed with your own eyes how he could defy the laws of physics. In one sense, you believe that he can do it, you have the proof that he can do it, but would you trust him to do it with *you*? Would you have put your own life in his hands such that he might accomplish with you what you could never do alone? It is said that the man who crossed with him was instructed to become as one with him. Contrary to his natural impulses, he was told to relax completely, to not at any point try to balance or assist, but simply to be at one with Blondin. If at any point Blondin's volunteer attempted to take a little control, the results would prove fatal for both of them.

This illustration shows us what is meant by faith in Jesus. We might know what Jesus can do and we might have even seen Him do it in the lives of others. But will we, like them, relax into His embrace and surrender all control of our lives to Jesus, such that He might carry us back to God, traversing with us the vast chasm that our sin has opened up between us? Faith requires that we let go of our desire to prove our own righteousness before God and instead let Him take the reins in our lives, since only God can save us. If we say that we have faith in Him, then let us put ourselves wholly in His hands. When we cry out to God for mercy, knowing ourselves to be helpless without Him, then this is exactly what we do.

The great paradox here is that as we relinquish all control to Jesus, we step into a glorious liberty. When we are taught to believe that salvation depends on us, then religion becomes burdensome and our service of God becomes fearful. We begin to worry about whether or not we have done enough to please God. But such thoughts have no place in the life of a genuine believer. The follower of Jesus does not live in fear of future damnation, but rather lives in gratitude for sins forgiven. The primary attitude of Christian worship is loving thankfulness and certainly not fear. As St John reminds us, *'There is no fear in love, but perfect love casts out fear; for fear has to do with punishment, and whoever fears has not reached perfection in love.' (1 John 4:18, NRSV)* Although our repentance might begin with fear of damnation, and although we should never lose a sense of the awesome majesty of God who is a 'consuming fire' (Hebrews 12:29), as we come to know God, we discover that we are made children in His family and that His primary attitude towards us is love.

Jesus' heart was broken at the sight of so many people left without the careful and sacrificial shepherding they needed from their leaders. He could see how the poor leadership of the religious authorities was crushing the people. One time He accuses the Pharisees of heaping all sorts of demands on the people, of burdening them with rule after rule after rule, and then doing nothing to help them meet their expectations (Matthew 23:4). To those made weary by such expectations, Jesus says:

> *'Come to me, all you that are weary and are carrying heavy burdens, and I will give you rest. Take my yoke upon you, and learn from me; for I am gentle and humble in heart, and you will find rest for your souls. For my yoke is easy, and my burden is light.' (Matthew 11:28-30, NRSV)*

This is an invitation Jesus extends to us too. The picture Jesus draws is an agricultural one. Imagine an ox pulling a plough through heavy soil, or else straining to shift a cart laden with hay. The ox is a powerful animal but over-burdened and left to work alone, it will soon tire and fall to the ground. But when two oxen are yoked together, suddenly their strength is multiplied, such that their capacity is greater than that of two single oxen working separately. The word yoke was often used in Jesus' day to speak of a body of instruction, and here Jesus makes a contrast. The ministry of the Pharisees resulted in people burning out spiritually in their attempts to fulfil stringent religious demands in their own strength; is it any wonder so many gave up. But the yoke of Jesus is an easy yoke and His commandments are light. The joy of submitting to Jesus' yoke is that Jesus walks alongside us, He has already yoked Himself to our humanity, and His strength greatly multiplies our own. In fact, so strong is Jesus, that to be yoked to Him is experienced as rest and, by the power that He supplies, the fulfilling of the commandments of God becomes far from impossible.

      The call to follow Christ is ultimately a call to participate in the very life of God, a participation made possible by the coming of God among us in order to unite Himself with our human nature. In Jesus, we are reconciled to God and through faith we are bound to Him. It is this binding, this becoming as one, that allows us to receive and live out the blessings of His death and resurrection.

Chapter 4

United to Christ

One of the things I enjoy most about ministry is journeying with others as they explore the Christian faith either for the first time or after many years of distance from the life of the Church. One day I received a phone call from an Iranian man declaring that he wanted to get baptised and become a Christian. Matthew (not his real name) told me of how he had been turned away from many churches already, probably because they were suspicious about his real intentions. But I agreed to meet with him. His friend and colleague, who had become a Christian several years earlier, brought him to church and after the service we talked. I sensed a sincerity in his desire to convert, if not a complete understanding of what it means to become a Christian. So, I told him I would be happy to baptise him, but only if he was happy to undergo a fairly rigorous preparation. Delighted, he agreed.

Over the next few months, Matthew and I would meet weekly to explore the Christian faith. One day as we were exploring the death and resurrection of

Jesus there was a moment when I can say that the penny finally dropped. You could see on his face what an impact the good news was having on him as he understood for the first time the full import of the Church's teaching about Christ and his cross. It was a beautiful moment, one of those moments you remember all your life, and as Matthew finished taking it all in, he said, 'Well, if that's how it is, then why would anyone not want to become a Christian? It's beautiful, it makes so much sense.'

Later that year we were preparing for the day of Matthew's baptism and, for the first time in the history of our church (as far as I am aware), we filled up a paddling pool so as to make sure he was properly immersed. This was to be his completely new start with Jesus. The day of Matthew's baptism came and the bishop arrived to take the service since Matthew would also be confirmed. The bishop was excited too, and what followed was a remarkably moving service in which this young Iranian man, who had been turned away so many times, finally made his public declaration of faith in Jesus Christ who would never turn him away. But perhaps the most breath-taking moment was the baptism itself. The bishop stepped into the paddling pool alongside Matthew and let out a high-pitched squeal (the water was not warm by any means), and he instructed Matthew to kneel down in the water beside him. Then, invoking the name of the triune God, Father, Son, and Holy Spirit, the bishop pushed Matthew under the water. At that moment Matthew came up from the water looking a little stunned. Afterwards I asked him how it felt and he told me the most remarkable thing. Matthew said that as he went under the water, he felt as if he wanted to cry out but he could not. His heart stopped beating and he felt as if he had literally died. I suggested that it might have been the cold but Matthew, who was used to swimming in the cold sea, said it felt different. And then, as he came up, he felt himself to be a new creature, completely new. What is even more interesting is that he has not smoked a cigarette since. Quite spontaneously that old habit died in the pool as the old Matthew was immersed in the waters of Baptism.

Matthew's story is probably not unique but it is incredibly special. In fact, every time someone gives their life to Jesus, parties break out all over heaven. Matthew's testimony of a very palpable death and resurrection should not shock us or strike us as bizarre because that is exactly what baptism is supposed to be, a death and resurrection. From the days of Jesus right through until the present day, baptism has normally been, and should properly be, administered by full immersion. The current practice in many churches today of sprinkling or pouring over a font has more to do with convenience than anything else and fails to convey the spiritual nature of baptism in its entirety.

The Anglican Church's definition of sacraments is that they are an outward and visible sign of inward and spiritual graces; that somehow the action performed represents and gives materiality to an event in the heart that cannot be seen with the eyes. The tradition of full immersion is important because it reminds us of the total surrender of the whole self to Jesus, of the need for the whole of our humanity to be washed by the waters of regeneration and for the old sinful nature to be drowned. The idea of pressing the candidate down under the water for a brief moment is intended to symbolise the drowning of the old man with all of their sin and corruption, such that they might be raised a new creation with Christ. When we are baptised, the old nature is buried in the waters, just as Christ was buried in the tomb, and when we are lifted up from the depths, we share in the regenerating power of the resurrection. All of this is an action made effective by the Spirit of God through faith in Jesus Christ. St Paul writes:

> *Do you not know that all of us who have been baptized into Christ Jesus were baptized into his death? Therefore we have been buried with him by baptism into death, so that, just as Christ was raised from the dead by the glory of the Father, so we too might walk in newness of life.*

For if we have been united with him in a death like his, we will certainly be united with him in a resurrection like his. (Romans 6:3-5, NRSV)

The whole idea is that through baptism into Christ and, therefore, in union with Him we are enabled to share in His very death and resurrection and, through participation in His saving acts, be set free from the power of sin and death such that we might literally begin a new life with God.

In the third chapter of John's gospel we encounter Nicodemus. Nicodemus was a Pharisee (John 7:50) who comes by night to speak with Jesus. Many have wondered why Nicodemus would choose to come under the cover of darkness. Maybe he thought this would be the best time to catch Jesus alone, or perhaps he was afraid of being identified with someone who was already beginning to ruffle the feathers of the religious authorities. Nicodemus' first words are warm and congenial: *'Rabbi, we know that you are a teacher who has come from God; for no one can do these signs that you do apart from the presence of God.' (John 3:2, NRSV)* Clearly, he respects Jesus and sees that somehow God's hand must be at work in Him. He cannot deny the gracious signs performed by Jesus' and he recognises in Jesus' teaching and actions the very presence of God. Nicodemus is sensitive to God and he is willing to come and learn from Jesus.

Jesus recognises in Nicodemus a man of spiritual integrity, someone He can get straight to the point with. So, He skips over the pleasantries and says: *'Very truly, I tell you, no one can see the kingdom of God without being born from above.' (John 3:3, NRSV)* Understandably, Nicodemus is confused. He recognises that Jesus is speaking of a new birth, but his mind is still bound by natural thinking. *'How can anyone be born after having grown old? Can one enter a second time into the mother's womb and be born?' Jesus answered, 'Very truly, I tell you, no one can enter the kingdom of God without being born of water and Spirit.' (John 3:4-5, NRSV)* Nicodemus cannot quite see how anyone can truly start again. We are born once and cannot go back to the beginning. Surely, what is done is done. But Jesus' declaration is startling: yes, we can go back to the beginning and, unless we do, we can never enter God's Kingdom. But this new birth is not a fleshly birth as our first birth was, rather it is a work of the Holy Spirit in us, a spiritual rebirth expressed through baptism.

On the day of Pentecost, St Peter preaches the Church's first sermon to the multitude. This crowd had gathered to see what all the commotion was about when the Spirit of God had fallen on the disciples gathered in the upper room. After Peter's impressive sermon many of his listeners were deeply affected and began to ask, *'Brothers, what should we do?' (Acts 2:37, NRSV)*, and Peter responds, *'Repent, and be baptized every one of you in the name of Jesus Christ so that your sins may be forgiven; and you will receive the gift of the Holy Spirit. For the promise is for you, for your children, and for all who are far away, everyone whom the Lord our God calls to him.' (Acts 2:38-39, NRSV)* Clearly, the central call to all who would follow Christ is 'repent'. Repentance is the foundation stone of discipleship and without it not even the ritual of baptism can be effective, it would not be an outward sign of the reorientation of the heart towards God. Our first call is to repent, to return to God and to rely on His strength for our salvation. Then we are called to be baptised, to undergo a symbolic washing as Christ, by the power of the Spirit, washes us clean of every spot and stain of sin, such that we might be forgiven our sins and enter into a renewed relationship with God. Similarly, at the end of Mark's gospel, Jesus says to his apostles: *'Go into all the world and proclaim the good news to the whole creation. The one who believes and is baptized will be saved; but the one who does not believe will be condemned.' (Mark 16:15-16, NRSV).* Again, we see the connection between baptism and faith, between the public washing of the penitent and belief in Christ into whose life the believer is baptised.

Our baptism is nothing short of a baptism into the very life of Christ. As we are united to Christ through faith, what belongs to Him by nature becomes ours by grace, and we are made children, adopted sons and daughters in the household of God, with all of the rights, privileges and responsibilities of those who call God Father. As we are untied to Christ in His death, our old nature with all of its sins and transgressions is nailed to the cross and buried in the tomb with Jesus. The old me dies. Spiritually, we are crucified with Christ and the death which came into the world on account of our sin no longer has any hold on us (Galatians 2:19). We have a fresh start, a new beginning. As St Paul writes: *'if anyone is in Christ, there is a new creation: everything old has passed away; see, everything has become new!' (2 Corinthians 5:17, NRSV)* This new start, this new birth, is entirely an act of God, it is 'by the Spirit' and entirely by His power. When we turn to Christ He puts His Spirit within us; we are baptised in the Spirit and, as St Paul reminds us, *'if the Spirit of him who raised Jesus from the dead dwells in you, he who raised Christ from the dead will give life to your mortal bodies also through his Spirit that dwells in you. (Romans 8:11, NRSV).*

The whole of the Christian life is based on a continued participation in the life of God. Our growth in holiness is entirely by the indwelling power of the Spirit of God, given to those who believe, and our ability to draw close to God and to live lives worthy of His name comes entirely through our sharing in the life of Christ. St Paul went so far as to say that *'it is no longer I who live, but it is Christ who lives in me. And the life I now live in the flesh I live by faith in the Son of God, who loved me and gave himself for me.'*

(Galatians 2:20, NRSV) To walk faithfully with God is to live by Christ's power and to seek daily to be strengthened in Him. It is not to walk by our own strength and wisdom, but to learn to trust in and depend upon God's.

In the famous passage from John 15, Jesus expresses the utter necessity for his followers to remain untied to Him, and to live out of their fellowship with Him.

> *Abide in me as I abide in you. Just as the branch cannot bear fruit by itself unless it abides in the vine, neither can you unless you abide in me. I am the vine, you are the branches. Those who abide in me and I in them bear much fruit, because apart from me you can do nothing. Whoever does not abide in me is thrown away like a branch and withers; such branches are gathered, thrown into the fire, and burned. (John 15:4-6, NRSV)*

The first thing to notice is that this abiding in Christ is a commandment. It is something for which we have some responsibility and therefore is something we also have the capacity to give up. Abiding in Christ is a continued state, something we should seek to maintain, something Christ asks of us if we are to live from the life that flows from Him. Sure, we need the Spirit's power to remain united to Christ, and the Spirit is given that this might be so, but we must offer our will, we must consent to this abiding through intentional actions.

Then we are reminded that we can do nothing of lasting value for God unless we maintain this close relationship with Jesus. Just as the harvest of grapes depends on the branch remaining connected to the vine, so any harvest of righteousness and good works in our lives depends on our continued connection to Jesus. The whole life of a disciple flows from our relationship with Him, and our repentance is the very act by which we seek to maintain that relationship. Whenever we sense that we are pulling away from God, we make an about face and turn back to Him.

This image is also deeply relational, it is an intimate picture which suggests a connection between the believer and Christ in which the very life of the Christ is supplied to the believer. Should the believer be separated from Christ and His Church, Christ's power and Christ's life are not diminished, it is the one who falls away that withers up and perishes. This is a challenge for us to be intentional in our relationship with God, to let nothing come between us and to seek to live wholly by the energy that He provides, that we might bear fruit in our own lives for His glory.

In St Paul's letter to the church in Galatia, he speaks of the 'fruit of the Spirit', the kinds of characteristics that become evident in the life of a person who lives rooted in Christ: *'the fruit of the Spirit is love, joy, peace, patience, kindness, generosity, faithfulness, gentleness, and self-control.' (Galatians 5:22-23, NRSV)* These fruits are the fruits of the Spirit. They are entirely God's work in us. If we desire to be holy as God is holy and to pursue that holiness without which no one can see God (Hebrews 12:14), then we must live by the Spirit and not by our own human strength and power. In fact, only a few verses earlier, St Paul tells us what the fruit is of those who live by the power of the flesh: *'Now the works of the flesh are obvious: fornication, impurity, licentiousness, idolatry, sorcery, enmities, strife, jealousy, anger, quarrels, dissensions, factions, envy, drunkenness, carousing, and things like these.' (Galatians 5:19-20, NRSV)* If we have died with Christ through faith in Him and the work of His cross, then the flesh has been crucified with Him. Therefore, as those brought to new life through participation in His resurrection, we are called to live by the Spirit's power, to walk by the Spirit's leading and to work with God for our sanctification by His renewing grace.

Repentance is about letting go of our self-reliance and laying hold of the works of Christ. Repentance is, in part, the acknowledgement of the insufficiency of our own resources to bring about our own salvation and to develop a genuine holiness. Repentance takes such knowledge and combines it with the knowledge of God's love to form a trusting relationship in which we wean ourselves off independence and self-righteousness and instead throw ourselves entirely upon Christ and drink deeply of the living waters that He supplies.

Chapter 5

Saved for Good Works

I remember asking my congregation during a sermon one Sunday how we are saved. I was astounded to see just how many of my beloved people still thought we were saved by good works, by our own efforts. It is a common idea and the fact that so many believe it is not surprising given that pretty much every other world religion works on that basis. Whenever I talk about the Christian faith with people out and about in my parish, I am also struck by how most people who do not go to church also think of Christianity in these terms. *'I don't go to church but I'm a good person'*, is a statement I often hear. And if being good and not doing too many naughty things were all that Christianity was about, then, why indeed would you go to church? Surely that is just an optional extra for the super keen.

The question about the place of good works in the Christian faith has raised many debates over the centuries, some of them quite heated. We have seen already how the Bible teaches that we are saved by grace through faith in Christ Jesus. So what then are we to do with good works? Can we even say that good works have a role to play in our repentance, or is repentance a once for all moment in a person's life completely unrelated to how we live day to day? I would like to suggest that good works are an integral part of our repentance. Although we are not saved or even justified before God on account of our own personal merits, good works are essential in the Christian life and not optional.

In his letter to the Ephesians, St Paul writes:

For by grace you have been saved through faith, and this is not your own doing; it is the gift of God— not the result of works, so that no one may boast. For we are what he has made us, created in Christ Jesus for good works, which God prepared beforehand to be our way of life. (Ephesians 2:8-10, NRSV)

St Paul is emphatically clear that there is nothing of which we can boast in relation to our redemption other than in Christ through whom God grants us salvation as a free gift of His grace. Indeed, he goes on to express how anything that we become following our conversion is entirely a work of God's hands. Indeed, the good works that follow are the fruit and not the cause of our redemption; they are the fulfilment of the very life for which we have been saved. In short, we have not been saved by our good works, but we are certainly saved for good works, and we are called in Christ to be fruitful in His service.

In the gospels, Jesus explains that a tree is known by its fruit. He tells us that a good tree bears good fruit and a bad tree bears bad fruit, and that one cannot bear the other.

> *No good tree bears bad fruit, nor again does a bad tree bear good fruit; for each tree is known by its own fruit. Figs are not gathered from thorns, nor are grapes picked from a bramble bush. The good person out of the good treasure of the heart produces good, and the evil person out of evil treasure produces evil; for it is out of the abundance of the heart that the mouth speaks. (Luke 6:43-45, NRSV)*

Notice how Jesus relates the quality of the fruit in our lives to the condition of our hearts. There is a connection between the inner life of a person and their outer life, between their inner world and their outer world. Certainly, there can be no fruit until the tree has first sprouted, put down roots, matured, flowered and been pollinated; and so just as the tree must always come before its fruit, so good works are the fruit and not the cause of our life in Christ. Further, the fruit which is good comes from a heart that is right with God. Fruit in a believer's life is the consequence of first being united to Christ, just as the branch must remain in union with the vine if it is to yield a harvest. Good works are the fruit of our salvation, and the evidence that all is working properly inside of us.

St James' letter in the New Testament is a deeply practical epistle, filled with instructions on how to lead a godly life. In many ways it is reminiscent of the Sermon on the Mount, in which Jesus Himself gives us a lengthy sermon on what a pure and godly life looks like. Jesus did not shy away from calling His followers to live lives filled with good works and He put a great stress on a purity of life that goes far deeper than surface appearances. There are many who are so scared of undermining the beautiful doctrine of salvation by grace alone, that they almost cut out the role of good works in a believers' life. But Jesus' teaching is deeply practical and we see this practicality continued in St James' letter. In one of the classic passages on this subject he writes:

> *What good is it, my brothers and sisters, if you say you have faith but do not have works? Can faith save you? If a brother or sister is naked and lacks daily food, and one of you says to them, 'Go in peace; keep warm and eat your fill', and yet you do not supply their bodily needs, what is the good of that? So faith by itself, if it has no works, is dead.*
>
> *But someone will say, 'You have faith and I have works.' Show me your faith without works,*

and I by my works will show you my faith. You believe that God is one; you do well. Even the demons believe—and shudder. Do you want to be shown, you senseless person, that faith without works is barren? Was not our ancestor Abraham justified by works when he offered his son Isaac on the altar? You see that faith was active along with his works, and faith was brought to completion by the works. Thus the scripture was fulfilled that says, 'Abraham believed God, and it was reckoned to him as righteousness', and he was called the friend of God. You see that a person is justified by works and not by faith alone. Likewise, was not Rahab the prostitute also justified by works when she welcomed the messengers and sent them out by another road? For just as the body without the spirit is dead, so faith without works is also dead. (James 2:14-25, NRSV)

St James encourages us to see that a living faith, which is the only kind of saving faith, is shown to be alive by the good works that it produces in our lives. Yes, faith in Christ's works is what saves, but that faith cannot be called faith if there is no change in our lives. If there is no change, then can we really say that we have been renewed in Christ? St James is confident that his works will be the proof of his faith, just as fruit reveals the nature of the tree that bears it. St James goes on to suggest that our works are the completion of our faith, just as Abraham demonstrated his faith in God by living obediently to Him. Faith and obedience to the commandments of Christ go hand in hand, and obedience to Christ's commandments testifies to the truth of our repentance, showing that we have indeed given Him our allegiance. It is for this reason that when commissioning His disciples at the end of Matthew's gospel Jesus says: *'Go therefore and make disciples of all nations, baptizing them in the name of the Father and of the Son and of the Holy Spirit, and teaching them to obey everything that I have commanded you.' (Matthew 28:19-20, NRSV)* Obedience is an essential element of our discipleship and should follow on naturally from our baptism into Christ's life. How can we say we have fellowship with God and share in His life if our impulse is to disobedience and not to righteousness?

John the Baptist was a great preacher, one of those fire and brimstone types who did not pull his punches. One day whilst preaching to the religious leaders of his day he said something that helps us to understand the place of good works in our repentance.

> *But when [John] saw many Pharisees and Sadducees coming for baptism, he said to them, 'You brood of vipers! Who warned you to flee from the wrath to come? Bear fruit worthy of repentance. Do not presume to say to*

> *yourselves, "We have Abraham as our ancestor"; for I tell you, God is able from these stones to raise up children to Abraham. Even now the axe is lying at the root of the trees; every tree therefore that does not bear good fruit is cut down and thrown into the fire. (Matthew 3:7-10, NRSV)*

Straight away we see that the lack of good fruit and holiness in our lives has eternal consequences. But John is not preaching that we are saved by being good. Quite the contrary. Many of John's contemporaries had a false confidence before God based on their prestigious ancestry. They would have said that by virtue of being descended from Abraham they could count on a place in the Kingdom of God as a sort of birth-right. This is like saying, *'I'm saved because I go to church'*, or, *'I'm saved because I was born in a Christian country'*. It is a view of salvation that requires me to take no personal responsibility. I suspect that John wants to warn them that the baptism for which they come is not a mechanical process like purchasing a ticket for a dinner party. Baptism is to be the sign of a changed heart-orientation in which God becomes sovereign over the ego and in which God's ways hold sway over our own inclinations and desires. Bear fruit and make sure it is good fruit, this will be the test of the sincerity of your repentance.

This is not to say that we will never sin. This is not to say that once we are baptised into Christ and home to the indwelling Spirit of God that we will be perfect right from the outset. But what we are saying is that the nature of repentance is to renounce the ways of the flesh and the world that does not honour God, and to say yes to Christ's rule in our lives. The truly repentant soul takes a stand against the sin in its life and refuses to excuse it or make peace with it, knowing just how destructive it can be to its relationships with God and with other people. The truly repentant heart will not seek to justify sin, but will rather turn to Jesus for cleansing and for the justification that He gives, seeking the renewing power of God's Spirit to work within us the perfection that God requires.

St Paul speaks of this struggle in a rather personal testimony from his letter to the Romans:

> *'So I find it to be a law that when I want to do what is good, evil lies close at hand. For I delight in the law of God in my inmost self, but I see in my members another law at war with the law of my mind, making me captive to the law of sin that dwells in my members. Wretched man that I am! Who will rescue me from this body of death? Thanks be to God through Jesus Christ our Lord!' (Romans 7:21-25, NRSV)*

Notice how St Paul speaks of the struggle, of the war that wages within him. This is the evidence of his repentance, that the sins he sees still evident in his life grieve his heart. This clearly shows that he is one with the Holy Spirit, who is, in his holiness, grieved by our sin; it shows that St Paul is on God's side. St Paul also recognises that in his own strength he is powerless against the besetting power of sin, that his rescue comes entirely in Jesus, for whom he expresses profound gratitude towards God. If, then, we are serious about our own repentance then we too must not make our peace with sin. St Paul reminds us that the life of repentance is one to be lived daily, that in every moment evil lurks close at hand seeking to lead us away from Christ. Therefore, the life of repentance requires a continual vigilance and an attitude of defiance in the face of temptation. Jesus says: *'From the days of John the Baptist until now the kingdom of heaven has suffered violence, and the violent take it by force.' (Matthew 11:12, NRSV)* The life of a Christian is warfare and the summons of Christ is a call to arms. Therefore, all of us who belong to Jesus must actively pursue obedience, otherwise we shall find ourselves pulled backwards by the strong currents of the world around us that flow away from God.

Chapter 6

Obedience to Christ

We live in an age in which people talk so much about freedom. When many people speak of freedom what they often mean is the ability to determine what is right for their own lives, to make their own decisions and to go wherever their feet may take them. The idea, then, of freedom through obedience can seem something of a contradiction and even an aberration, an antiquated idea to be thrown out and destroyed. But this is precisely what the Christian faith proclaims: freedom through obedience, freedom in service to Christ. But how we understand freedom has a lot to do with how we understand the human person and what you think makes up the purpose of mankind. For a Christian, our purpose is God and our humanity is most complete when we are united to Him, living in perfect and uninterrupted communion with Him. We are made for worship and we are made for God. Therefore, we are most free, most human, most alive, when we worship and when our inclinations and desires move uninterrupted towards God. When our spirit moves in step with the Spirit of God, then we truly know life, for *'where the Spirit of the Lord is, there is freedom.'* (2

Corinthians 3:17, NRSV) But whenever we find ourselves asserting our own will over against the will of God then, naturally, we move away from Him and therefore turn our backs on the Lord and Giver of Life.

Obedience to the commandments of God is an act of profound trust. When we choose to submit to the teachings of Scripture, we are expressing our faith that God does indeed know what is best for His children and that to be shaped by His word, is to be fashioned after the likeness of the living Word, Jesus Christ. St John writes:

> *This is the message we have heard from him and proclaim to you, that God is light and in him there is no darkness at all. If we say that we have fellowship with him while we are walking in darkness, we lie and do not do what is true; but if we walk in the light as he himself is in the light, we have fellowship with one another, and the blood of Jesus his Son cleanses us from all sin. (1 John 1:5-7, NRSV)*

St John draws our attention to the absolute holiness of God. He is light, a light in which not a hint of darkness can be found. If this is the case, then He alone can be trusted to rule over us with perfect love, and in Him alone can all truth be found. Those who say they belong to God walk in the light, they walk under the lamp of God's word and submit to His ways. It is important to note here that St John links the washing away of sins by the blood of Jesus with our desire to share fellowship with the light. Obedience is the positive aspect of our repentance. As we renounce the sin in our lives and nail it to the cross of Christ, we turn to embrace the Gospel and to walk in faithfulness to God.

> *Now by this we may be sure that we know him, if we obey his commandments. Whoever says, 'I have come to know him', but does not obey his commandments, is a liar, and in such a person the truth does not exist; but whoever obeys his word, truly in this person the love of God has reached perfection. By this we may be sure that we are in him: whoever says, 'I abide in him', ought to walk just as he walked. (1 John 2:3-6, NRSV)*

For John there is an intrinsic connection between obedience and love. Obedience is the means by which we abide in the love of Jesus; obedience is the action by which we say yes to his saving work in our lives. He assures us that if we obey the commandments of God then we can be certain that He dwells within us and that we dwell in Him (1 John 3:24), and chief among those commandments is the command to love God and to believe in the Christ whom He has sent (1 John 3:23). So important are the commandments of God, that at the great commission, as Jesus sends out His disciples to preach the good news to all of creation, Jesus says: *'Go therefore and make disciples of all nations, baptizing them in the name of the Father and of the Son and of the Holy Spirit, and teaching them to obey everything that I have commanded you.' (Matthew 28:19-20, NRSV)* Disciples of Jesus are to be taught to obey everything that Christ has commanded. Desiring to be like Jesus is the essence of discipleship. How we respond to the question of obedience also exposes the place that God has in our lives. If we proclaim that Christ is Lord, then we must work to make sure that He has no rival in our hearts and that His summons triumphs over all the competing voices of this world that seek to draw us away from Him.

In a lengthy and difficult sermon about his flesh and blood, many of Jesus' followers began to desert Him (John 6). They found His words difficult and, not feeling they could accept them, they had no choice but to part company. Jesus did not change His preaching in order to court their favour or to win back their allegiance; the truth is the truth however people respond to it. Turning to his closest followers, Jesus challenges them, *'Do you also wish to go away?' Simon Peter answered him, 'Lord, to whom can we go? You have the words of eternal life. We have come to believe and know that you are the Holy One of God.' (John 6:67-69, NRSV)* Jesus' words are eternal life and they come from the fount of all holiness. Obedience to Jesus, no matter how difficult it is in this life, is always a choice for eternal life. This perspective is essential. We must always remember that to choose Jesus is always to choose life.

I see Christian obedience much in the same way that I see music. Every musician knows that in order to experience the full freedom of their art, with the endless possibilities for composition and melody, they must first submit to music's basic laws and restrictions. My children like to bash away on their toy keyboard. You could say that they are totally free, that since they are not bound by the rules of music, they can make whatever sounds they like. Granted, they are free from the constraints of music, but whatever they attempt to play, it invariably sounds the same, and more often than not consists mostly of jarring sounds and painful dissonance. I usually have to leave the room. If, however, they learnt their scales, practiced simple tunes and became familiar with reading music and keeping time, what would gradually emerge would be something altogether more beautiful and delightful. It is like this in our walk with God. Without His laws and the boundaries that He sets with His commandments, our lives would consist mostly of dissonance and the tendency to repeat the same mistakes and habits. But as we submit to His ways and humble ourselves before Him, so we discover an increasingly beautiful capacity to improvise, a freedom that brings great joy.

Chapter 7

The Necessity of Confession

I really do not like going to the dentist. The whole idea makes me anxious. In fact, I once went nearly seven years without so much as a check-up. If you were to ask me why I find the thought of the dentist so uncomfortable, I would probably say that I am afraid of being told there is a problem and I know from experience that problems in the teeth usually mean needles, drills and that horrid sensation of drowning when the dental assistant is busy looking out of the window. When I think about it, being afraid of going to the dentist does not make much sense at all, because the dentist is there to help me. The whole point of visiting the dentist is to keep my mouth healthy and to make sure that problems get dealt with before they cause lasting damage to my wonderful smile – and it really is wonderful, you can ask my wife!

Having put off the dentist for so long, it turned out that when I did finally get up the courage to go for a check-up, my gingival recession was pretty advanced – something which still makes me reluctant to look at my teeth in the mirror – and I also needed three fillings. In time, one of those fillings turned into a rather long and painful course of root canal and a short period of looking like I had been punched in the face by a prize fighter. How I wish I had plucked up the courage to go sooner.

Perhaps one of the dentist's most important tools is their spotlight. Without it they would struggle to get a clear picture of the state of my teeth and gums and those dark recesses would remain something of a mystery. Without the clear and searching light of the dentist, many infections and spots of decay would go undetected, only to then take hold and lead to tooth loss and much anguish. Then there would be much weeping and gnashing of gums!

The light of the dentist might not be comfortable, especially if it turns up a problem. But that light turns out to be our best friend because it alerts us to the need for action; it spotlights the problem and paves the way for something to be done about it. In that sense, it is a healing light. In John's Gospel, the evangelist tells us that Jesus came as a light into the darkness of this world:

> *And this is the judgement, that the light has come into the world, and people loved darkness rather than light because their deeds were evil. For all who do evil hate the light and do not come to the light, so that their deeds may not be exposed. But those who do what is true come to the light, so that it may be clearly seen*

that their deeds have been done in God.' (John 3:19-21, NRSV)

For those who love sin and have grown comfortable in their rebellion, the coming of Christ is a painful experience. Sometimes rejecting Christ and shying away from the light of His presence can feel more comfortable than facing up to the reality of our brokenness and seeing by the light of His holiness all of the spots, stains and wrinkles in our hearts that we would rather not know about. Ignorance is bliss for a short time at least. But for those who desire truth and who trust in God, those who desire to pursue holiness and righteousness, the light becomes our friend and the presence of Jesus in our lives wakes us up to our need for His saving grace.

God is gentle. Like an onion with all of its layers, or a Russian doll with all of its bodies, one tucked beneath another, the true me is buried under layers of sin. But God, by His sanctifying grace, strips us back one layer at a time, gradually revealing new layers of sinfulness, some of which might even surprise us, so that He might cleanse us and wash them away by His blood. But of course, like going to the dentist, this is a process we must embrace, a small death we must undergo for the sake of our healing and our perfection in holiness.

Taking responsibility for our sin and actively opening our hearts to the searching light of God's Spirit takes a certain humility. Yet those who desire God know that this stripping away of all the false pretensions and masks of the self that we have built up to hide away our sin, is indeed the means by with we are released to walk in the glorious liberty of the children of God.

In the book Genesis, just after Adam and Eve had tasted of the fruit that should not be eaten, God comes and speaks with them. First, He draws them out from their shadowy hiding place and, bringing them into the light, He asks them what they have done. *'Have you eaten from the tree of which I commanded you not to eat?' (Genesis 3:11, NRSV)* Immediately, Adam shifts the blame to Eve: 'She made me do it, she gave me the fruit'. But as God's attention shifts towards the woman, she then points the finger at the snake. Of course, God already knew what they had done, but He gave them the opportunity to own up, to claim responsibility for their sin and to make their repentance. Nevertheless, both Adam and Eve shift the blame, they refuse to take ownership of their wilful disobedience. I wonder what might have happened had they acknowledged their fault before God and cried out for His forgiveness.

So often we too look for people to blame, and waste so much precious energy pointing the finger at others, if not seeking to justify ourselves before others and before God. But unless we can see and acknowledge our own personal stake in this world's sin, then we will never find ourselves in the right place to repent and to receive the forgiveness of God. If we seek to justify ourselves before God, then we shall be found lacking because all of us have sinned and fallen short of His glory (Romans 3:23). Indeed, the only justification sufficient for our release from the consequences of sin is the justification that comes through faith in Jesus Christ. Repentance requires a certain degree of humility. Humility requires that we put to death the pride in our hearts which so often reacts against the idea of our own failure. We must humbly seek God for His mercy.

As I get older, the man in the mirror increasingly catches me by surprise. Occasionally when I stop to look at my reflection – which is not very often, honest - what I see is considerably more wrinkly and tired-looking than the picture I have in my mind. The reality of the reflection does not always bear much resemblance to the airbrushed version of my face that I carry around in my head, and the cold light of day compels me to take action, to invest in some moisturiser, to whip out the beard trimmer, and to eat more fruit for the sake of my skin.

I find that it is like this when I read the scriptures, but instead of showing me how much the children are aging me, they act as a spiritual mirror, reflecting back the true condition of my heart. Time spent in the Bible is time spent with Jesus and as I listen to and reflect on His words, they help me to get a more accurate picture of myself. When I look at Jesus, I see an image of true humanity and when I listen to His words and read the stories that tell of His deeds, I finally have a measuring stick by which to discern the extent to which I am living a full and holy life. So often the temptation is to measure myself against others, to point out and examine the faults of others and thereby convince myself that I am not quite as naughty as I really am. Or, worse still, I spend so much time weighing up others that I lose all sense of my own need for change. What we need is a solid and fixed measure of holiness, a true plumb line by which to discern the relative crookedness of our own hearts, and that plumb line is Jesus. *'The Lord said, 'See, I am setting a plumb-line in the midst of my people Israel''* *(Amos 7:8, NRSV).*

Seeing a vision of authentic humanity, revealed in Christ, alerts me to the fakery in my own soul. Similarly, being exposed daily to the revealed will of God in the words of the Bible gives me a point of orientation from which I can see how far I have wandered. Then, when my conscience is pricked and my sin is uncovered, I have an opportunity to seek God in confession and to receive His forgiveness, His healing and His love.

The psalmist writes:

> *Oh, how I love your law!*
> *It is my meditation all day long.*

How sweet are your words to my taste,
  sweeter than honey to my mouth!
Through your precepts I get understanding;
  therefore I hate every false way.
Your word is a lamp to my feet
  and a light to my path.
(Psalm 119:97, 103-105, NRSV)

A lamp. A light. In order to walk safely in the darkness of this world we must take hold of the Scriptures and walk by their light. The light helps us to see and the light keeps us from danger. Can we say that the light of scripture is our daily mediation, and that we find it to be sweet like honey in our mouths?

The Lord loves us and His desire is that we should repent and be saved. He has done everything necessary for our healing and for our redemption. He is the doctor, the dentist, who heals all our infirmities and cleanses us of every stain of sin. As we sit in the waiting room and hear Him call out our name, do we turn away in fear or do we receive the deliverance that He brings? Do we close our ears to His call and convince ourselves that there is nothing wrong, or do we allow Him to examine us more closely, that we might receive the sure and certain benefits of His life-giving death and resurrection? St John writes:

> *This is the message we have heard from him and proclaim to you, that God is light and in*

him there is no darkness at all. If we say that we have fellowship with him while we are walking in darkness, we lie and do not do what is true; but if we walk in the light as he himself is in the light, we have fellowship with one another, and the blood of Jesus his Son cleanses us from all sin. If we say that we have no sin, we deceive ourselves, and the truth is not in us. If we confess our sins, he who is faithful and just will forgive us our sins and cleanse us from all unrighteousness. If we say that we have not sinned, we make him a liar, and his word is not in us. (1 John 1:5-10, NRSV)

I think most of us know that we have sinned at some point or another. Even non-Christians speak of a conscience, a kind of inner compass that alerts us to the fact that we have strayed off course. Sadly, for some, the pattern of transgression is so deeply entrenched that their moral compass no longer seems to function, or else its signal has been jammed by the lead weight of sin in their hearts. Most of us, however, do recognise its signal and that signal alerts us to the presence of some kind of absolute standard, some universal sense of moral appropriateness that has been hardwired into us. St Paul suggests this when he writes:

> *When Gentiles, who do not possess the law, do instinctively what the law requires, these, though not having the law, are a law to themselves. They show that what the law requires is written on their hearts, to which their own conscience also bears witness; and their conflicting thoughts will accuse or perhaps excuse them on the day when, according to my gospel, God, through Jesus Christ, will judge the secret thoughts of all. (Romans 2:14-16, NRSV).*

For those of us who have already made a decision to follow Christ and who are already seeing the fruit of His healing and sanctifying work in our lives, our conscience, that sense of the rightness – or wrongness – of things, seems to grow stronger. I like to imagine that the conscience somehow relates to the image of God deep within us, the image of God in our spiritual DNA. When we sin, we live contrary to our true nature and our lives fail to match up with the template of God's likeness in our hearts. This discrepancy causes a sort of pain, a dissonance that informs our spirit that our lives are no longer in sync with God. The more that the image of God drawn within us is revealed in our lives and the more like Jesus we become, the more easily we see the discrepancies and the more keenly we feel the dissonance.

When we sin, especially when we willingly sin, perhaps by giving in to some temptation or other, it is quite normal to feel shame. Sometimes that shame can make us feel unworthy to turn to God in prayer. The purer we become in our hearts, the greater we feel the soiling after every sin, such that even smaller sins might leave us feeling miserable. It is not that the sin is any more destructive than before, only that a small speck on a white sheet stands out far more than it would on the compost heap. As we grow in holiness, we become more sensitive to sin's negative action in our hearts and it grieves us just as it grieves the Spirit of God (Isaiah 63:10; Ephesians 4:30). When we transgress the laws of love towards God and neighbour, we feel how it separates us from God and from others around us.

The enemy would exploit this shame. Sometimes, especially in those painful moments immediately following a particular transgression, he might begin to whisper to us that we are not fit to draw near to God. In fact, he might try to convince us that being so defiled we should not turn to prayer at all but rather wait awhile until we feel a little bit better; he might encourage us to wait until we have had a go at trying harder on our own, such that we might have some good works and a little effort to present to God.

But remember the attitude of the prodigal's father whose first thought was reconciliation with his long-lost son. Remember how he himself took responsibility for removing his son's soiled garments, to then dress him in his own fine clothes. Whenever we fall willingly into sin, whenever our conscience accuses us, whenever we discover by the light of the Spirit or by meditating on Scripture that we have in some way sinned against God's holy law, then we know that because of Jesus and God's love for us, we can confess our sins immediately to Him, and know the forgiveness that flows from the cross of Christ, where the price for every sin has already been paid.

The shame that we might feel on account of our sin can also become a great source of energy for repentance. Perhaps this is why the enemy would dissuade us from praying when the shame feels so strong. When we have a clear sense of our utter need of God's mercy and our helplessness without His sovereign grace, then we truly learn to trust in Him, then we truly discover how much we need Him and how insufficient are our efforts without Him.

In some traditions Christians are encouraged to go to confession. Sometimes confession is formalised with a set form of words and a specific arrangement of furniture. Sometimes it happens in the confidential security of conversation with a trusted brother or sister in Christ. Anyone who has confessed their sins before Christ in the presence of another believer, who acts as a sort of witness, will know that the act of confession requires considerably more courage and can feel a lot more painful than when we simply make a confession alone before God in our private prayers. It is not easy to lay bare our darkest secrets before another. But a good confessor does not judge. Rather a good confessor might offer some words of advice and encouragement before pronouncing the forgiveness of Christ that all of us are assured of if we humbly confess our sins before God. The effect is a powerful one. In that moment, when the sins of which we are most ashamed are met not with condemnation but with mercy and grace, how much sweeter do we feel the compassion of Christ and how much deeper do we appreciate the depths of His love. When we confess our sins, when a sinner repents, there is more joy in heaven than there is over a multitude that have no need of repentance.

The Psalmist expresses it so beautifully:

Happy are those whose transgression is forgiven,
  whose sin is covered.
Happy are those to whom the Lord imputes no iniquity,
  and in whose spirit there is no deceit.
While I kept silence, my body wasted away
  through my groaning all day long.
For day and night your hand was heavy upon me;
  my strength was dried up as by the heat of summer.
Then I acknowledged my sin to you,
  and I did not hide my iniquity;

> *I said, 'I will confess my transgressions to the Lord',*
>   *and you forgave the guilt of my sin.*
> *(Psalm 32:1-5, NRSV)*

Even in the Old Testament we hear preached the wonderfully good news that those who confess their sins to God will know His forgiveness. Christ's cross has made that forgiveness available to people of every age and every nation. And notice that the psalmist speaks of how silence over our sin and a failure to expose it to the light leads to sickness. Unrepentance is perhaps the worst sickness of all, for sin is the only disease that has eternal consequences. The call to confess is our call into the doctor's surgery, and the act of confession is the beginning of our healing. It is the first step into everlasting life.

Chapter 8

Tending the Field of the Heart

Perhaps one of the best-known and most-loved stories of Jesus is the parable of the sower (Matthew 13:1-9, 18-23; Mark 41-9, 13-20; Luke 8:4-15). It is a story that has time and again moved me to confession and repentance. In this story, Jesus uses an everyday picture from the agricultural setting around Him, in order to help us look more deeply into our own hearts and to see with a greater clarity our receptivity to the words and works of God. This is one of the few parables for which Jesus provides an explanation that has been recorded for us in Scripture, and so in some ways it is easy for us to understand and, as we understand it, we come to understand ourselves more fully.

One day a farmer goes out into his field to sow some seed. You can imagine Jesus and his listeners looking across the hillside to such a scene as this. The farmer scatters his seed across the ground with a sweeping movement of the arm and the seed lands all around him. Some of that seed falls on the path. The soil is hard, trampled down by years of footfall and almost as soon as the seed hits the ground the birds swoop down and gobble it all up. Some of the seed falls on soil that is shallow and filled with stones. That seed sprouts and shoots up quickly, but since the soil is shallow and the roots cannot run deep, the scorching sun burns up the plants and they soon wither up and die. Other seeds fall on soil that is deep enough but nevertheless filled with weeds. The thorns and thistles grow up alongside the wheat and because of competition for nutrients, space and sunlight, the crop fails to yield its harvest, having been choked out by the weeds. Finally, some of the seeds land on good soil, deep and weed free. This seed grows to its full stature and offers a harvest, some ears yielding thirty, some sixty and others a hundredfold.

Many have observed that this should really be called the parable of the soils. The seed is the word of God sown in people's lives and the soil represents the hearts of those who hear it. As we hear the story we are encouraged to reflect on our own response to God's word and see which soil best fits our own spiritual condition. In the story the farmer sows the seed. In each case the farmer is the same, his action in sowing is the same, and the seed is the same, each seed holding the same potential for life and for fruitfulness. There is no failure on God's part. He sows His word liberally and generously, allowing it to land in all sorts of places. The seed that lands on the path is reminiscent of when the word of God is sown in a person's life but immediately the enemy comes and snatches it away. The heart of that person is so hard and unreceptive that the enemy need not work too hard to make sure it never finds a home there.

There are many things that can harden a heart to the word of God. One of these is pride. Pride sets itself up against God and is blind to its own failing. A heart that is proud exalts itself above God and above other people and this has the effect of straining and damaging our relationships with God and with others. When we look down on others or presume to know better, when we deny the truth that we too have sinned against God and others, then we take a stance in our hearts that is devoid of the grace and humility that we see in Jesus and we become incompatible. Pride keeps us from acknowledging and confessing our sins, and it prevents us from shedding the tears of repentance by which our hearts are softened and made receptive to the healing and sanctifying grace of God. The proud heart sees no need of God's mercy and seeks only to justify itself, thus shutting itself off from the justifying work of Christ. The proud heart has more in common with the enemy and so the enemy gains sufficient ground to devour the faith of those who will not walk humbly before God.

Hearts can also be hardened through habits of wilful sin. Whenever we sin, we wound our hearts and just as skin that is wounded regularly becomes hard and inflexible through scaring, so too the heart becomes calloused and hard through the effects of regular and wilful transgression of God's holy ways. The more we sin, the more insensitive we become to the things of God and the harder it becomes for God's word to penetrate into our hearts where it may put forth shoots and bear fruit for His glory. If we are intent on continuing in sin, then we have made a decision against Christ and the result is a certain hardness towards him.

Wilful sin also includes hardness towards others. When we refuse to forgive and harbour grudges and resentments, then we trample down our own hearts too, such that we damage our own fellowship with God. Jesus was clear that our forgiveness of others is a fruit of the repentance by which we receive the mercy of God.

What is our attitude towards others and towards God? Do we sense in any part of our lives a certain arrogance or pride that inhibits the free flow of love between ourselves and others? Is there a sin in our lives with which we have made our peace, something we have excused or justified, such that we regularly and willingly go against the commandments of God? Do we find that as we read God's word or hear it preached that it is as if it bounces straight off us and disappears? If this speaks to where we are at now, then maybe this is a time to pause and to ask God to reveal the areas of hardness in our hearts and their causes, and to help us, by His grace, to soften the soil such that His word might find a home in us.

The seed that fell on the shallow soil reminds us of when the word of God is received gladly but any resulting faith is short-lived. Sometimes I come across people who tell me that they used to go to church or that they used to believe in God but now do not. More often than not it was pressure from without that caused their faith to wither so soon and to die. Perhaps it was the struggle to nurture their faith whilst living in a family that was neither sympathetic nor open to Christianity. Sometimes it was the pressure of the world around them to relegate worship and times of prayer and spiritual refreshment to an afterthought, something not to be practiced if it interfered with 'real life'. Sometimes, outright hostility and persecution have simply uprooted the fledgling Christian before they could ever get going. Quite often it was some personal tragedy, some illness, or the loss of a loved one that opened the door to a barrage of doubts and frustrations which in turn conspired to undermine their newfound faith in Christ.

Interestingly, in Jesus' story the heat that causes these seeds to wither and die is the same heat that causes the good seed to grow and ripen. Persecutions and hardships are there for all believers, for those with a deep and rich faith and for those with little or no faith at all. In the one instance, the 'heat' of life releases energy for growth and maturity, whilst for others it leads to the destruction of faith. The difference here is not the conditions within which we live, neither is it even the challenges that seek to weaken our faith, namely the issue is the depth of our relationship with God and the extent to which our faith penetrates deep into our lives.

When our faith is shallow, we cannot expect it to withstand the trials and tribulations of life. When our faith is little more than attending services or going through the motions or the casual turning to God when it suits us to do so, then we cannot expect it to last in the face of the many pressures that life presents to all of us. If our faith in Jesus is more about what we get than it is about giving glory to the God of heaven, then it is easy to see how it might wither in moments when it feels as if life is not going our way.

In Jeremiah, the prophet presents us with a beautiful picture of the ways in which cultivating a deep faith, rooted and grounded in God, can help us to flourish and bear fruit, whatever the weather in our lives.

> *Blessed are those who trust in the Lord,*
>   *whose trust is the Lord.*
> *They shall be like a tree planted by water,*
>   *sending out its roots by the stream.*
> *It shall not fear when heat comes,*
>   *and its leaves shall stay green;*
> *in the year of drought it is not anxious,*
>   *and it does not cease to bear fruit.*
> *(Jeremiah 17:7-8, NRSV)*

The call of the disciple is to sink our roots deep into Jesus who is for us a stream of living water. These roots are strengthened and deepened through those regular habits of prayer and worship, through an intentional seeking of intimacy with God and a prioritising of the time to be refreshed in His presence.

The word of God is also enabled to go deeply into our hearts when we allow it touch every area of our lives. Jesus said that the Kingdom of God is like when a woman takes a lump of leavened dough and mixes it in with a whole batch of fresh dough, such that the whole lot is transformed by the action of the yeast (Matthew 13:33). The more we knead the word of God into our lives and the more we surrender of ourselves to Jesus, the stronger we become in Him. As followers of Jesus we are called to allow His word to affect all our decisions and actions, our thoughts, our words, the way we spend our money, the manner we take with other people, the ethics we live by at work and the attitudes we harbour towards others. These are just a few examples of areas of our lives we can and should submit to the word of God.

As we reflect on this soil, how deep would we say that our faith runs? How faithful are we in cultivating that deep intimacy with the Lord of Life, such that the stresses and pressures of life become for us opportunities for growth and maturity in the faith, and not the rocks by which it is shipwrecked? Can we say that we have surrendered the whole of our lives to God, or are there areas of our lives that we have not allowed to be touched by the word of God? Do we separate out parts of our lives that we do not think have anything to do with God?

The next soil is deep enough for the seed to grow properly and it is certainly not starved of nutrients, but it is crowded. Alongside the wheat there are all sorts of weeds which leave little room for the crop to yield a harvest. In this instance, all of the worries of this life and the various pleasures and treasures that it offers take over the inner life of the believer such that there is little room left for the word of God to grow. Consequently, faith is not able to mature and bear fruit. In Matthew 6, in the middle of the Sermon on the Mount, Jesus warns against worrying. It is something we are all prone to do if we are not careful, and we know that when worry takes hold it is hard to think about anything else. Jesus encourages us to be intentional about seeking first the things of the Kingdom and prioritising God's righteousness. This is not to say that the things we need such as shelter, clothing and food do not matter, but that our primary attitude towards these things should be rooted and grounded in our knowledge of who God is and how much He loves us. These meditations should foster within us a sense of trust towards God that diminishes worry.

And why do you worry about clothing? Consider the lilies of the field, how they grow; they neither toil nor spin, yet I tell you, even Solomon in all his glory was not clothed like one of these. But if God so clothes the grass of the field, which is alive today and tomorrow is thrown into the oven, will he not much more clothe you—you of little faith? Therefore do not worry, saying, "What will we eat?" or "What will we drink?" or "What will we wear?" For it is the Gentiles who strive for all these things; and indeed your heavenly Father knows that you need all these things. (Matthew 6:28-32, NRSV)

Interestingly, this passage follows on from Jesus' words on the idolatry of greed (Matthew 19-24). Jesus warns against storing up wealth and prioritising the treasures of this life. He likens the pursuit of earthly riches to a kind of slavery which renders us incapable of serving God, for a slave can only serve one master. Jesus instructs us to consider what is our greatest treasure because the thing we love most is the thing to which we will give our hearts. If, then, our hearts are given over to worry or else to the lusts and pleasures of this life, how can we ever hope to mature in Christ and see His fruit in our lives? The space just is not there.

As we reflect on the soil filled with weeds, can we see a reflection of our own condition? Are we prone to worry, or to doubt the providential care of God? Do we find that we struggle to leave things in God's hands after we have commended them to Him? Is there perhaps some treasure in this life - money, fame, popularity, sex, food, television, work – that crowds out our inner space, such that we lose all thought of God and find ourselves distracted in our walk with Him?

At the end of the parable, Jesus shows us just how fruitful the life of a disciple can be when our hearts are soft to Him, when our faith runs deep and when we do not allow any rivals to our affection for Christ. Such a life is marvellously fruitful and gives great glory to God. Such a life is the fulfilment of our humanity and yields a joy beyond compare. Jesus says: *'My Father is glorified by this, that you bear much fruit and become my disciples.' (John 15:8, NRSV)*

One of the things I love about my garden is watching it mature. I love seeing how the garden changes throughout the seasons, but I also get a thrill from seeing how the garden grows and matures over the years as some plants die whilst others grow bigger and stronger. I also have lots of self-seeding plants that pop up in all sorts of unexpected places, lending the garden a certain spontaneity. But I also know the importance of weeding. Keeping a good garden is not just about the constructive action of selecting the right plants and placing them within the wider scheme; keeping a good garden is also about the hard work of weeding out the invasive and destructive presence of weeds and removing plants that are not where they should be. In fact, this second work is so important that nearly all of my labour in the garden is given over to it, far more time and effort than is spent planning and planting.

When we first moved into our house the garden was quite plain and at the back there was a large overgrown area where the previous occupant had attempted a wildflower border. I guess what they had hoped for was something reminiscent of a cottage garden, with a certain kind of disorderly beauty, that would not need much work. In reality, what they got was a lot of doc, brambles, grass and dandelions. The problem was that the preparations had not been thorough enough, neither had there been sufficient attention paid to maintain what had been created. Some gardeners go to extraordinary lengths to clear their soil of weeds. With a good riddle and much patience, they will spend hours sifting through the whole garden such that every alien root or stone might be removed. The whole point is to make sure that there is nothing buried beneath the soil that might one day rear its ugly head to spoil the garden. Furthermore, even a well sifted garden must still be hoed and weeded regularly otherwise new weeds will arrive and slowly the garden will be once more given over to chaos.

Our hearts are like gardens and their soil needs tending. The quality of our hearts and the kinds of thoughts and feelings that we allow to take root there will influence the overall effect of our words and deeds. If our hearts are filled with thoughts of sin and are all tangled up in the brambles of worry and materialism, for example, then we can hardly expect our lives to reflect the beauty of holiness and reflect the likeness of Jesus. Tending and sifting through our thoughts and feelings and keeping a close watch over our hearts is an expression of the repentance that leads to life. James writes, *'rid yourselves of all sordidness and rank growth of wickedness, and welcome with meekness the implanted word that has the power to save your souls. But be doers of the word, and not merely hearers who deceive themselves. (James 1:21-22, NRSV)* Like gardeners tending their borders, we are to watch over our inner life, receiving the good seed of God's word and allowing it to influence our very living, whilst all the while ridding ourselves of everything that threatens to spoil its growth in us.

I have watched over the past year or two as my new next-door neighbour has struggled to find a gardener to tend her garden with diligence and care. One time I watched as one particular gardener attempted to get control over the weeds that had taken over the borders. He hacked away with his spade and by the time he had finished the overall effect was impressive. The garden looked amazing and once more the beautiful rich soil could be seen between the various shrubs and flowers. The man took his money and made off. Unfortunately for my neighbour, this man had not dug deep. All he had done was skim the surface and remove the appearance of the weeds, but their roots were left intact, lurking beneath the soil, ready to sprout again. Within a couple of weeks, the garden looked awful.

Our repentance must be thorough and regular and whenever we recognise the presence of sin, we must take drastic action to destroy it at its root. We must ask God's Spirit to show us how deep it goes and cry out to God for the grace to see it removed from our lives. It is tempting to judge the state of our hearts by our outward appearance, but the scriptures remind us that God looks deep within to the very core of our being, and that it is what he finds on the inside that matters, because it is possible to keep the appearance of sin at bay, whilst allowing it free reign beneath the surface.

This was exactly the charge that Jesus laid against the Pharisees. The Pharisees were a religious elite who had made themselves professionals of holiness, devising and keeping all manner of religious laws. By all accounts they looked to have everything together spiritually; they did and said all of the right things. But Jesus could see deeper.

> *'Woe to you, scribes and Pharisees, hypocrites! For you are like whitewashed tombs, which on the outside look beautiful, but inside they are full of the bones of the dead and of all kinds of filth. So you also on the outside look righteous to others, but inside you are full of hypocrisy and lawlessness. (Matthew 23:27-28, NRSV)*

A whitewashed tomb is a thing of beauty and judging by its outward appearance who would suspect that within it you could find a heap of rotting bones and the stench of decay. These are the words with which Jesus challenges us to make sure that our holiness is not a sham or a show, but a reality that touches the very depths of our being.

As those who take our repentance seriously, we must seek daily to keep our hearts free from sin. Whenever we see it, we should pluck it out and allow all the space we can for the things of God to fill our inner vision. This might seem like drudgery to some, but the reality is far more beautiful than anyone might imagine. A well-tended garden is a thing of wonder, and properly presented and given the right conditions, each plant is enabled to shine in its place. So too, each virtue in the life of a believer is able through careful tending to shine out for God's glory, and the whole effect of the believer's life is to fill the air with the sweet fragrance of Jesus. Furthermore, the heart that is clear of sin is able to behold God more fully than otherwise, and to see God, to gaze upon the beaty of His face and know His presence is nothing short of eternal life. Jesus says, *'Blessed are the pure in heart, for they will see God.' (Matthew 5:8, NRSV)*

Chapter 9

Attending to our Minds

The repentant life is a response to Christ's call for us *'to love the Lord your God with all your heart, and with all your soul, and with all your mind." (Matthew 22:37, NRSV)* The reality is that we do not, but we know that we should and we also know that to live in union with God is the fulfilment of our humanity and the source of all true joy. The life of discipleship is in many ways a retraining of our faculties to respond positively to Jesus and to react strongly against sin. The whole of our personhood has been affected by the fall but, as we have seen, the whole of our personhood has been united to God in Christ. Therefore, every part of us can be renewed and redeployed in the service of God. It is interesting that when Jesus calls us to love God, he calls us to do so not just with our souls and hearts and bodies, but also with our minds. The mind is a key battleground in the spiritual struggle and it is in the mind that we are often most vulnerable to the insinuations of the evil one. It is in the mind that temptations first appear and the mind is where the battle is often won or lost. As those who are serious about repentance, we must take time to think about the kinds of things we think about. Understanding how the mind can be engaged, or disengaged, in our spiritual struggle can make all the difference in the outcome of our fight against sin and temptation.

The scriptures have a lot to say to us about our mindset. Our mindset is the basic attitude or orientation of our mind and the scriptures speak about the mind as something over which we have a certain degree of control. The Christian disciple is called to have a mind fixed on Jesus, a mind that is turned to Him and set in His ways and not set in its own ways. In Philippians, St Paul urges us to have the humble mind of Christ in our dealings with one another (Philippians 2:5). The attitude of our mind matters.

The first question to ask ourselves is which influences have the biggest impact on shaping the way that we think. Maybe we have never considered the fact that the way we think will be shaped by the environments in which we live and the things we choose to feed our minds with. It follows, for example, that if we spend a lot of time watching violent films or playing violent computer games, we might become desensitised to the violence in the world around us and may even become more violent in our own thoughts and actions. That is an extreme example, but it may be that our views and our ways of approaching particular issues are formed by the company we keep or by the kinds of newspapers that we read. There is a battle going on for our minds and if we are not mindful of the different influences that bear upon our minds, we might find ourselves with a mindset that reflects more the spirit of the age than that of the Spirit of God.

> *'I appeal to you therefore, brothers and sisters, by the mercies of God, to present your bodies as a living sacrifice, holy and acceptable to God, which is your spiritual worship. Do not be conformed to this world, but be transformed by the renewing of your minds, so that you may discern what is the will of God—what is good and acceptable and perfect.' (Romans 12:1-2, NRSV)*

In this passage, St Paul is not only concerned that we present our bodies to God to be used in his service with purity and love, but also that we should consecrate our minds to Him. The suggestion is that there is a fundamental opposition between the way that the world thinks and the way in which God thinks. When St Paul speaks of 'the world' he means that part of creation that has not surrendered to the lordship of Christ and which therefore stands in opposition to Him. St Paul recognises that the basic attitude of the world is not like that of the true follower of Jesus and so he warns us to be mindful of the difference and to make sure that the temperature of our hearts is not set by the spiritual temperature of the world around us, but rather by Christ Himself. The question is this: do we think more like Jesus or do we think more like the people in this world who do not know or love Him? When we read the Bible, do we find that it resonates with us and that its counsels are like music to our ears, or do we find that it challenges and contradicts the ways we prefer to think? As we have seen, repentance literally means a change of mind and St Paul makes the incredible claim that the changing of our mindset is crucial for our transformation into the likeness of Christ.

The mind is like a muscle. It can be trained. It can be made stronger or else it can be left to grow weak and flaccid. If we are used to allowing our minds to work in a certain way, it can be difficult to change how we think but becoming aware of the need for change is half the battle. In Proverbs 21:31 we read, *'The horse is made ready for the day of battle, but the victory belongs to the Lord.' (NRSV)* This perhaps best sums up the part we play in our spiritual struggles: we put on our armour, we plan and we act, but the strength to fight and the victory itself comes by the Spirit's power. So, we can begin by confessing our failings of the mind and seeking God's grace for renewal.

But how do we re-train the mind? Well, like training a muscle you have to use it. The more you use it in a certain way the easier and more natural it becomes. The more you resist thinking in a way that dishonours God and the more you seek to think in a manner worthy of Him, the more natural it becomes for us to think like that. It is for this reason that St Paul can tell us to *'Set your minds on things that are above, not on things that are on earth, for you have died, and your life is hidden with Christ in God.' (Colossians 3:2-3, NRSV)* As those whose lives have been hidden away with Christ in God, it is not fitting for our thoughts to be consumed by the things of this world, neither is it fitting for us to reason like those who resist the very mind of God. Setting our minds on Christ is a choice that is ours to make.

If it is true that the books we read, the programmes we watch on the television, and the kinds of conversations we share have an impact on shaping our mindset, then it follows that cultivating a godly mindset might involve the kinds of things we feed it with. In his letter to the Philippians, St Paul exhorts the community with these splendid words: *'Finally, beloved, whatever is true, whatever is honourable, whatever is just, whatever is pure, whatever is pleasing, whatever is commendable, if there is any excellence and if there is anything worthy of praise, think about these things.' (Philippians 4:8, NRSV)* He calls us to meditate on the things that move us to worship, to love, and to prayer; he commends to us the practice of not dwelling on the ugly, the profane or the outright sinful. If I use a bucket to carry manure, then I cannot be surprised if it begins to reek of the undesirable; but if I then begin to use that same bucket to carry pure water, eventually the bucket will become clean. What, I wonder, are we filling our buckets with?

If we are to taste the joy of a truly repentant lifestyle, then we must recognise that this not only involves renouncing that which soils our thinking, but also means embracing and feasting on that which lifts our minds to God. Jesus reminds us that it is the cleanliness of our hearts that matters to God and that a source that is polluted cannot yield works that are pure and pleasing to Him: *'what comes out of the mouth proceeds from the heart, and this is what defiles. For out of the heart come evil intentions, murder, adultery, fornication, theft, false witness, slander.' (Matthew 15:18-19, NRSV)* If our actions are sinful, then the source of that sin lies within us.

What can be said then of temptations? Even should we become pure within, just as Christ was pure and without sin, we could still expect to suffer temptations, just as Christ was tempted in the wilderness. As with developing a gospel mindset, dealing with temptations is something that requires practice and endurance. The enemy is devious and has thousands of years' experience in leading people to sin, and he knows how to disguise our temptations such that by the time we realise what is happening we are well on our way towards sinning, if not already regretting something. He knows which temptations will be most effective against us.

For this reason, attending to our minds is not simply about keeping them clean and well weeded, but also about protecting them from outside attack. Most of us are not used to keeping vigilance over our thoughts and have grown accustomed to letting thoughts wander in and out of our heads as they desire. We pick them up, not questioning where they come from, and we play with them, turn them over, look at them and talk to them. Often a single thought can snowball into an all-consuming desire, a full raging row either in our heads or actually with another person, or else it can leave us feeling guilty or unloved. Our fantasies and daydreams and the thoughts we choose to give our attention to influence our behaviour and make it either easier or more difficult to resist sin.

In this sense, tempting thoughts are like door-to-door salesmen. I remember as a child hiding with my mum behind the sofa because we had seen someone coming up the drive who would be difficult to shake off. The man in question pressed the door bell, waited a little, and getting no response, left to try on someone else's door. That was a shrewd move. How often we wished we had checked through the spyhole before opening the door. The easiest way to avoid buying something you do not want from a doorstep peddler (apologies if that is your profession, but please bear with me) is to not even open the door in the first place. It is the same with thoughts. When a thought approaches, we can have a look at it and make a decision, whether it is something we really want to be thinking about, or even if it is something Christ would want us to be thinking about. If not, then we turn our attention elsewhere until it goes away.

If the thought persists, we must be strong. If we open the door, all is not lost, but things will get a little more difficult. Like the salesman, the thought will seek to stir our interest and draw us into conversation. It will begin to show us its wares and encourage us to handle them and see for ourselves how delightful they are. It is getting harder to resist, but we can still say 'no thank you' and shut the door. But what if we let the thoughts in? Then it gets trickier. They will get comfortable and begin to unpack all sorts of other things we did not know they had with them, and now the living room of our mind is filled with all sorts of stuff we could really do without. It will now be difficult to get the thoughts out without a great deal of fuss, after all we have actually just given them permission to come in. By now, they are well on the way to persuading us to do exactly what they want us to do and buy into their suggestions. Despairing we might feel that the only way we can get the temptation to leave is to give in, thinking that only then will we be left alone.

In short, we must learn to check our thoughts before letting them in, and the earlier we can spot their true nature, the easier we will find it to expel those which are not of God. The longer we engage with tempting thoughts, whether they be thoughts of anger, lust, pride, anxiety, greed, or whatever, the harder we will find it to deal with them. In my own personal experience I still have a long way to go, but increasingly, the more time I spend being conscious of my thinking and being watchful over my mind, the more easily I see temptations coming, and the sooner I see them coming the more quickly I can take action.

Sometimes the best way to fight is to run for cover. If I know someone who is bigger and stronger than me, I might well ask them to fight on my behalf, and I know no-one bigger or stronger than Jesus. If we discover that we have let a temptation into our minds and the conversation is well advanced, we can cry out to God for His mercy and turn to prayer or worship. If we see the thought approaching but have not yet let it in, then we can make sure that we seal our minds with prayer and turn instantly to God. My spiritual director once told me that when he is beset by a particularly strong temptation, he turns to prayers of thankfulness. He begins to recall out loud everything that God has done for him, and he allows his gratitude towards God in that moment of weakness to move his heart to repentance. In this act of humility, the devil cannot follow because in his pride he is unable to abase himself before God. In this same vein, we must also be sure to guard against the subtleties of pride. If we find that we are making progress with our thoughts, we should be careful because the very thought of our progress might lead to self-congratulation, which usually opens the door to let in the very sins we have done so well resisting. We must thank God for every victory and ascribe all glory and honour to Him.

Someone might complain that all of this is a little over the top. It might be said that this level of care in our living is unnecessary, but the testimony of Scripture speaks to the contrary. In Matthew chapter five, Jesus shows us that bad thoughts are sins in embryo form. If we mean business in dealing with sin then we must see that the struggle is waged in our hearts. In fact, if we get our inner life in order, then our actions will soon follow suit. Jesus teaches us that if we harbour anger towards another in our hearts then we have already committed murder in our hearts. How often have we daydreamed of someone getting their comeuppance? If we are honest, we know that such thoughts betray a lack of love. Equally, if we lust after another in our imaginations, then we are already flirting with adultery, and that is certainly not of God either, and the more we entertain the notion, the more likely it is to occur. On this topic Jesus says: *If your right eye causes you to sin, tear it out and throw it away; it is better for you to lose one of your members than for your whole body to be thrown into hell. And if your right hand causes you to sin, cut it off and throw it away; it is better for you to lose one of your members than for your whole body to go into hell. (Matthew*

5:29-30, NRSV) The call is to take drastic action against sin because sin is the only disease that has the power to wreck our eternity. Even the worst of bodily afflictions end with death, but sin is the very door through which death comes into the world. As we seek to live in purity, the gospels call us to develop an eternal perspective.

Chapter 10

Spiritual Disciplines

When I was at university, I decided to try my hand at rowing. I had never considered it before, but the boat club did a pretty good job at recruiting new members. I can remember attending the introductory presentation to which I had been invited only to be given plenty of reasons to give up before I had even started. The president of the boat club spoke about the dedication that would be required to stick it out. He told us that within two weeks he would expect half of us to have given up, and even fewer of us to make it through our novice year. In time he proved to be right. The problem for many was that rowing was not something you could do casually when you felt like it; either you were in or you were out. Training was intense and even at beginner's level we were training at least six times a week, sometimes very early in the morning. My levels of strength and fitness rocketed and those who were not making the commitment soon fell behind. Rowing is also a team sport and when one person does not pull their weight, then the performance of the whole boat is affected. Further, you could not just call in sick if you did not fancy another session on the river because if you did not turn up, then the rest of the crew could not row. There were no half measures. It demanded huge amounts of commitment and rowing had to be your priority.

The word to describe all of this is discipline. Rowing, like most sports, takes discipline, especially if you want to improve. There was much joy in rowing, especially when out on the river in the frost at sunrise, but, at the end of the day, all that sweat and sacrifice was geared towards something greater, namely race day. All of those hours on the rowing machine or down at the gym were about training and strengthening the body for racing against other teams, not just to race, but to win. St Paul had made these observations when considering the sportsmen of his day.

> *Do you not know that in a race the runners all compete, but only one receives the prize? Run in such a way that you may win it. Athletes exercise self-control in all things; they do it to receive a perishable garland, but we an imperishable one. So I do not run aimlessly, nor do I box as though beating the air; but I punish my body and enslave it, so that after proclaiming to others I myself should not be disqualified. (1 Corinthians 9:24-27, NRSV)*

St Paul speaks of the athlete's self-control exercised in all areas of life, and all in the hope of winning a race. He speaks of discipline, of punishing the body, not for its own sake, but for the sake of glory. Then he compares himself to an athlete. But unlike those whose eye is fixed on a perishable garland of laurel leaves and the transient adoration of men, St Paul's eye is fixed on the crown that awaits him in heaven, the crown that lasts forever, and the great 'well done' of his heavenly Father. The point is quite simple: that we should see ourselves like athletes and exercise self-control in our spiritual lives. If people will go to such efforts disciplining their bodies in order to win a running race, how much more should we bring our whole bodies under control in order to finish the race we have begun in Jesus. The call to follow Jesus is a call for total commitment.

The Christian life involves discipline. The Christian life can be tough and as followers of Jesus we must do everything we can to make sure we stay the course. Repentance itself must be our daily concern because too often we fall away from God in our thoughts and actions. Much like my first boat club president, Jesus told his disciples: *'The Son of Man must undergo great suffering, and be rejected by the elders, chief priests, and scribes, and be killed, and on the third day be raised.' Then he said to them all, 'If any want to become my followers, let them deny themselves and take up their cross daily and follow me. For those who want to save their life will lose it, and those who lose their life for my sake will save it.'*

(Luke 9:22-24, NRSV) Jesus wants us to be clear about the cost of discipleship and He does not relegate the stuff about sacrifice to the small print. Jesus is up front and honest with us about what is required, and the sense He gives is that it will not be easy to follow in the footsteps of a crucified king. It is all or nothing, in or out.

Therefore, spiritual disciplines have always had an important role to play in the life of a believer. They are not about impressing anybody, neither are they about impressing God. The Church does not teach that by fasting or prayer or acts of loving service that we earn God's favour or merit forgiveness, neither do we encourage bodily mortification as an atonement for our sins; Jesus has already suffered for our failings and it is in His righteousness alone that we stand before God. With our spiritual disciplines we are not buying or selling anything. But our disciplines are instead designed to strengthen the inner man for prayer and holiness; it is a kind of training of our spiritual muscles and reflexes such that we can live for God with greater strength and love.

The writer of the letter to the Hebrews in his great chapter on faith tells the stories of numerous heroes of the Old Testament who trusted in the promises of God, many of which they would never see fulfilled during their lifetimes. He commends their faith and creating a picture of a great arena, filled to bursting with all of the saints of ages past, he writes:

> *Therefore, since we are surrounded by so great a cloud of witnesses, let us also lay aside every weight and the sin that clings so closely, and let us run with perseverance the race that is set before us, looking to Jesus the pioneer and perfecter of our faith, who for the sake of the joy that was set before him endured the cross, disregarding its shame, and has taken his seat at the right hand of the throne of God. (Hebrews 12:1-2, NRSV)*

Like St Paul, his exhortation is to run with perseverance and to cast aside everything in our lives that may weigh us down or trip us up. In all of this our focus must be on Jesus in whose footsteps we run. Like St Paul, this writer speaks of a joy worth running for and a prize for which it is worth committing everything. It was this mentality by which Jesus endured the cross and suffered every hardship, knowing that through perseverance in His Father's will He might reign forever at God's right hand and raise countless multitudes with Him to glory.

We live in a world that, for the most part, is apathetic towards Jesus, or else outright hostile to those who belong to Him. The cultures in which we live and the society in which we work and socialise are on the whole operating on a wavelength different from that of the Kingdom. Therefore, our spiritual lives need constant attention. If we stop swimming we get pulled back by the current, and therefore even to take a break is to lose ground. Similarly, if we neglect to use our spiritual muscles they will waste away; we either use them or lose them. By the same token, the more we exercise our faith and seek to strengthen our spiritual reflexes, the stronger and more effective they become.

Being a Christian is also a team sport, and we are baptised into Christ whose body is the Church, our community of faith. Whenever we are negligent in our walk with God, the whole body is weakened, but whenever we become stronger in our faith, the whole Church benefits. We owe it to each other and not just to ourselves to be strong in Christ; our spiritual disciplines are as much about the whole Church as they are about us. When we become more patient or self-controlled, for example, then we contribute to an atmosphere in our church fellowship in which it is easier for others to be patient and self-controlled.

Spiritual disciplines include regular times of prayer and devotion, and times of worship both together with others and alone. They might also include acts of loving-kindness and generosity, regular confession, fasting, or abstaining from particular pleasures for a time. We might also think of spiritual reading and other means of feeding our minds with healthy spiritual food. After all, an athlete's diet has a great impact on their performance. This list is not exhaustive, and perhaps you have your own examples. Spiritual disciplines are a valuable tool in our repentance. The desire to strengthen our bodies, minds and spirits for the spiritual struggle is a signal that we are serious about Jesus and serious about the life that He gives. Training of the spiritual muscles and reflexes assists us greatly in the fight against sin and it helps us to pursue that holiness required for encounter with the living God (Hebrews 12:14).

Take fasting, for example. Food is good in itself and God has created us to eat and enjoy the fruits of the earth. But gluttony is a perversion of our natural desire to eat and comes about when a person allows themselves to be ruled by their bellies. It is the same with sex, something beautiful and God-given that can be corrupted by lust when used to serve selfish ends such as self-gratification. This is not the way it should be; our bellies and all the other desires of the flesh are to be ruled by our wills, which in turn are to be ruled by the Spirit of God. Gluttony, for example, turns the whole thing on its head, such that the one who overindulges their inordinate desires will in turn become a slave to them and will begin to struggle with prayer and times of communion with God. We cannot serve two masters and, if we are slaves to our bodies, then how can we ever hope to be obedient to Christ. Comfort is perhaps the greatest god of our age, but if comfort and indulgence become the focus of our lives, then how can we ever hope to stand when obedience to Christ calls us to lay aside earthly delights and to endure hardship for His sake?

Fasting does not change our relationship with God directly, but it is a discipline by which we learn to exercise a certain degree of control over our desires, such that we can turn our wills towards things of greater value. Many times we fail, and I know how often my own fasts have ended sooner than expected. But each time we struggle to resist the urge to indulge a bodily passion, the stronger our wills become and the easier it gets. Many of us are not used to resisting our desires and sometimes it takes a great act of the will to do so. If our will is untrained for righteousness, then it can feel near impossible for us to follow Jesus and obey His commands when our own impulses are compelling us to walk away from Him. By strengthening our reflex to submit to Christ in times of peace through disciplines like fasting, we shall be equipped and strengthened to fight victoriously in the day of genuine struggle. Becoming stronger in one area will help us to become stronger in others. Disciplines like fasting are a sort of training for righteousness.

The athlete also takes great care to make sure that they are not carrying excess weight either in their bodies or on their bodies. They will keep their bodies lean and free from excess fat, as well as choosing clothing that is not too heavy and enables freedom of movement. In ancient times athletes would compete naked for this very reason, literally stripping themselves of every impediment. The same should be true for us who have already been admonished to *'lay aside every weight and the sin that cling so closely' (Hebrews 12:1, NRSV)* Spiritual disciplines enable us to lighten our hearts and to keep ourselves spiritually agile, such that we can live sensitively and responsively to the leading of the Spirit of God. Those who seek to bring their whole self into their repentance, turning every faculty back towards God, find that their prayers become stronger and their times of communion with God increasingly more fruitful, and this is ultimately what it is all about, fuller communion with God.

In all of this, however, we remember that self-control is a fruit of the Spirit. Although we take a little turn towards God by such actions, it is God Himself who comes the whole way to meet us, and it is by His grace alone that we are brought to perfection. Unless our disciplines are rooted in a trusting dependence on the enabling grace of God, they will do nothing but make us proud and lead us further from Him. The world is full of religions and religious people who trust in their spiritual practices and who aspire to great ascetic feats in their hope to reach perfection by their own efforts. Such disciplines are destructive and although they appear to speak of sanctity, they are not born of the humility that belongs to Christ. Whenever we fail in our disciplines, we humbly ask God for His mercy and seek His grace to persevere; and whenever we make progress, we thank God for the indwelling presence of His Spirit, without whom we could not even take one step towards Him.

Chapter 11

Attitudes Towards Others

> *'The first [commandment] is, "Hear, O Israel: the Lord our God, the Lord is one; you shall love the Lord your God with all your heart, and with all your soul, and with all your mind, and with all your strength." The second is this, "You shall love your neighbour as yourself." There is no other commandment greater than these. (Mark 12:29-31, NRSV)*

The commandments of God can be summed up with the word 'love'. Love is, according to Jesus, the fulfilment of the law. As his people, our call is to live outwardly, with hearts that stretch away from the self towards God and towards others. In the modern world we have lost the sense of our inherent connectedness with each other. We often speak of ourselves as individuals, but the idea of the 'individual' is a relatively new idea in the history of human society. The idea that we are all separate entities, like little atoms bouncing off one another, is a product of the Enlightenment. The idea that we are somehow separate and have to work towards unity with each other by artificial means is alien to the world of Scripture. In reality, humanity already possesses an essential unity, but that unity has been broken by the fall and through sin we have ruptured that sense of connection with each other. For this reason, it perhaps feels more natural to think of ourselves as separate individuals.

But we are not individuals, we are persons, and persons are people in relationship. We are most fully human when in relationship with others. After all, we are made in the image of the triune God, in whose one divine nature we see a plurality of persons: one God, three persons, Father, Son, and Holy Spirit, a communion of love, an interplay of dynamic, self-giving relationship. This is our natural pattern. Jesus comes to restore that essential unity to mankind and that unity is restored in Him. On the night of the last supper, Jesus prays: *'I ask not only on behalf of these, but also on behalf of those who will believe in me through their word, that they may all be one. As you, Father, are in me and I am in you, may they also be in us, so that the world may believe that you have sent me.' (John 17:20-21, NRSV)* In the Creed, when we profess our belief in the one, holy, catholic and apostolic Church, we are saying that the Church really is one in Christ. But then we look around and see the divisions within our own fellowship and the hostilities between denominations and ask if it really can be true. When the Church fails in love and unity is not seen, it is not so much that believers are not one in Christ, but that those who belong to the one Church of Christ are not living true to their nature as those brought together in Him.

It is the same with holiness. We proclaim the Church to be holy and yet we do not have to look very far to see how far we fall short of this ideal. The truth is that the Church is holy because it is the temple of the Holy Spirit of God, but when we sin, we are failing to live true to our nature as those who belong to the God of holiness.

When we learn to think of ourselves, as the Bible does, as somehow connected to one another, then we realise that there is no such thing as private sin. We suddenly become aware that my private and personal choices and the sins that I think affect no one but myself actually add to the burden that weighs down on humanity. By the same token, when I pray, when I make movements in love and humility and seek to pursue a deep and lasting union with God, then the whole of humanity is helped, and my so-called private devotions render a great service to the world. These thoughts should inspire us to greater personal holiness and to strengthen our commitment to prayer. They should help us into a greater sense of commitment towards one another. Is it any wonder that Jesus called the Church into being as the environment within which we are supposed to grow in Christian maturity? The Church consists of a new family, filled with people we did not choose to rub shoulders with, but whom we are nevertheless called to bear with in love and for whom we carry a certain responsibility as co-labourers in the vineyard of Christ.

It is in this sense that we perhaps get closer to what Jesus means when he says 'love your neighbour as yourself'. In the modern era, with all of the rampant individualism that surrounds us, it is natural to interpret this verse along the same lines as the self-help manuals which fill our bookshops, preaching a doctrine of 'balance' or self-love. We put the focus on loving the self as much as we love others, or at least seeking to love others as much as we love ourselves. This is not a bad thing, but I wonder of it goes deep enough. I wonder whether the deeper and perhaps truer sense is something like 'love your neighbour as if they were actually you'. In this vision, my own wellbeing is inextricably bound up with the wellbeing of others. The emphasis is then on loving others and relaxing into the knowledge that to be poured out for others is for my own wellbeing too. That is when I am most fully human, that is when I am most fully alive, when I am poured out for others, just as Christ poured himself out for me.

This reading seems to reflect more faithfully the witness of Jesus whose own life was an offering for many, and whose life should be the pattern of all authentic human relationships. St Paul makes this clear when he gives instructions on marriage.

> *Be subject to one another out of reverence for Christ.*
>
> *Wives, be subject to your husbands as you are to the Lord. For the husband is the head of the wife just as Christ is the head of the church, the body of which he is the Saviour. Just as the church is subject to Christ, so also wives ought to be, in everything, to their husbands.*
>
> *Husbands, love your wives, just as Christ loved the church and gave himself up for her.*
>
> *(Ephesians 5:21-25, NRSV)*

I love how marriage is presented to us as a martyrdom of love, each spouse surrendering to the other out of mutual love. The husband's love, for example, is to be patterned after the love of Jesus, who laid down His life for the Church. The fulfilment of this most personal and beautiful of relationships is dependent on the complete sacrifice of the ego and the complete commitment to see the other flourish. This is the ideal. Marriage is seen by the Church as a context within which man and wife can be perfected in love. As the couple wrestles with their shortcomings and perseveres in patience and forbearance, so holiness grows, and the crucible of marriage becomes the training ground for greater love and sacrifice in all our other relationships. This is why we speak of marriage enriching society.

But sin would destroy the unity between us that is part of God's purpose in our lives and the reality for which we were made. Sin not only disrupts our relationship with God but also our relationships with each other. This is why forgiveness matters and why the cross carries a reconciling power, because not only does the cross unite heaven and earth, but as we see Christ's arms stretched wide, He is drawing the peoples of the earth together into His embrace.

One day St Peter asked Jesus how many times he should forgive someone who offended him. In those days three times would have been considered pretty generous and so Peter, perhaps trying to impress Jesus, asks if seven times is enough. Jesus smiles and responds, not seven times, but seventy times seven times. In other words, let there be no limit to your forgiveness (Matthew 18:21-35). Then Jesus tells a story. He tells of a king who one day decided to put his affairs in order and called to him all those who owed him something. One servant owed him an astronomical sum of money, billions and billions of pounds. There was no way he could repay it and so the king ordered that he and his family should be sold into slavery to repay the debt. Understandably, the servant falls to the ground and pleads for mercy. Surprisingly, the king decides to pardon him, he simply lets him off the hook.

But then, on his way home, the servant comes across another servant who owes him some money;

not billions of pounds, but perhaps a couple of hundred. Filled with anger he puts his hands around the other servant's throat and demands to be paid at once. The poor servant falls to his knees and, like the first servant had done, he pleads for mercy, promising to repay everything that he owes. But unlike the king, the servant who had been forgiven so much shows no mercy and throws the second servant into prison. Of course, word gets back to the king who is furious and demands an explanation. He cannot believe that the man he had forgiven so much could bring himself to forgive so little for another. That first servant is handed over to the jailors for his punishment. Jesus finishes by warning us that we too must forgive generously from the heart.

The point is clear. We are like the first servant. God has forgiven us so much. He has cancelled our debts in Jesus simply because we cried out for mercy, and now He expects us to share of the forgiveness with which He has blessed us so liberally. When we refuse to forgive the sins of others who have hurt us, then we are like the unforgiving servant, showing that the kindness of God has not moved us to repentance.

It is not always easy to forgive, especially when the pain that someone has caused us runs deep. But forgiveness is still what Jesus asks of us. After all, forgiveness is in the nature of the King in whose kingdom we live. *'For if you forgive others their trespasses, your heavenly Father will also forgive you; but if you do not forgive others, neither will your Father forgive your trespasses' (Matthew 6:14-15, NRSV)* Refusal to forgive is nothing short of disobedience.

There is a danger that we confuse our will with our feelings. This can be dangerous in the spiritual life, so is it any wonder that the enemy has worked hard to create a culture within which we are encouraged to conflate the two. We are told, 'follow your heart', and, 'if it feels good it must be OK'. Certainly, we cannot always help how we feel, but our feelings are supposed to be subject to our wills and not the other way round. If we are driven by how we feel, then our lives will tend towards selfishness and thereby begin to fray our relationships with others. But if we can learn to exercise our will irrespective of how we might be feeling, then beautiful things can happen. Part of the repentant life is to recognise that for too long we have followed the devices and desires of our own hearts instead of submitting to the just and life-giving rule of God. Jeremiah reminds us that *'The heart is devious above all else; it is perverse — who can understand it?'* (Jeremiah 17:9, NRSV)

Jesus, as both man and God, had two wills: a human will and a divine will. But in Jesus the human will was completely conformed to the divine will, such that His whole life was one single movement of obedience, even unto death. We see this at Gethsemane where Jesus prayed before his arrest *'My*

Father, if this cannot pass unless I drink it, your will be done.' (Matthew 26:42, NRSV) Jesus clearly does not feel like going through the agony of the cross in order to pay the price for human sin, but He wills to do it because He knows that this is the Father's gracious plan. Jesus willingly offers up His life, in spite of the very real pain He would suffer, because His love of God and His love for God's people runs so much deeper than His love for Himself. Sometimes the call for us to take up our own crosses is a call to forgive what seems unforgivable.

Perhaps one of the most challenging passages in the Gospels is when Jesus instructs His followers to *'Love your enemies, do good to those who hate you, bless those who curse you, pray for those who abuse you. (Luke 6:28, NRSV)* It completely cuts against the grain of the world in which we live and yet this is the royal way of Christ. Prayer is a wonderful thing and I find it helpful that Jesus commands us to pray for our abusers in the same sentence that He tells us to love our enemies. When we pray for someone, we are essentially lifting them up to God for his healing and blessing. It is an act of love. A few years ago, I was subject to behaviour that left me fearful and afraid. The archdeacon instructed me not to answer the phone or even to go to the front door until it was resolved. When I thought of the man behind the actions, I felt no love towards him, only anger and fear. But I decided to pray for him anyway. And as I began to pray for him, God slowly began to change my heart, such that one day I realised that I was not angry anymore, but rather sad that he was in this state. I did not feel like forgiving him at first, but I chose to pray for him regardless and God took care of the rest. As Christians we are called to submit our wills to Christ, trusting that our feelings will catch up in due course. In seeking to love that man, as weak as my love may have been, I experienced a deep sense of release, freedom and peace.

Christ's attitude towards the sins of others is principally one of compassion. It was for love's sake that Jesus came and died for sinners, such that they might be restored to relationship with God. Sin is a disease and the various things we call sins – theft, anger, lies, violence, etc. – are really symptoms of a deeper sickness of the heart. When someone hurts us, their actions betray the presence of sin; but if we are honest, we also suffer the effects of sin in our lives, causing pain to others more often than we recognise. It might be that the symptoms of sin in someone else's life are less socially acceptable than our own, but sin is sin and all of us have fallen short of God's glory. It can help us to have a clear vision of our own need of God's mercy and a deep appreciating of the forgiveness we have received. When we cultivate that sense of humility before God and before others, we begin to see not an enemy, but a fellow sufferer, someone who is afflicted in much the same way as we are. All of us are in need of the saving and sanctifying work of God. Slowly, our attitude moves from anger to pity, and from pity to compassion. The fathers of the Church have always used the measure of our love for enemies as the yardstick for our spiritual progress, because love for enemies touches the very heart of Christ and reflects His attitude towards the world.

It can be helpful to build prayer for our enemies into our daily cycle of prayer and, if we cannot bring ourselves to pray for those who abuse us, we can ask God to give us His heart of compassion for the world, that we might learn to see those we struggle to love with His eyes. The same goes for when we are tempted to judge another's sin. It might be someone we do not know, someone we see on the news or someone we hear about in conversation. It might even be the foibles of those we work with or encounter throughout our day, but in each case the temptation to judge is one that can be hard to resist. In His parables of the Kingdom, Jesus reminds us that judgement belongs to Him and to the angels, and that should we begin to pass judgement, through our lack of discernment, we might misjudge and cause damage to others (Matthew 13:24-30). Christ's challenge to us is to attend to our own sins and not to worry about those of others:

> *'Do not judge, so that you may not be judged. For with the judgement you make you will be judged, and the measure you give will be*

> *the measure you get. Why do you see the speck in your neighbour's eye, but do not notice the log in your own eye? Or how can you say to your neighbour, "Let me take the speck out of your eye", while the log is in your own eye? You hypocrite, first take the log out of your own eye, and then you will see clearly to take the speck out of your neighbour's eye.' (Matthew 7:1-5, NRSV)*

The implication here is that whilst we too are grappling with sin, we lack the clarity of vision to carefully and lovingly help another with their sins. When we judge another person, we harm our brother or sister, and through passing judgement strengthen the pride that works to harden our own hearts towards others and towards God. This hardness, as we have seen, undermines our repentance and if we are not careful, we begin to cut ourselves off from the very mercy we have failed to extend towards others. When we show mercy in the face of another's sin, we demonstrate that repentance is at work within us. We are not saying that sin does not matter, or that we should make peace with the sin in another person's life; rather we are expressing the desire not to fight against others, but rather to stand alongside them in our common fight against our common enemy, just as Christ has come to stand alongside us, fighting in His strength for our freedom.

Chapter 12

A Heart of Praise

Repentance is not just an action but an attitude of the heart. Repentance describes a whole life that yearns to be where God is and to do what God would have us do. It is so much more than a one-off moment, or the reciting of a simple prayer at our conversion; it is nothing less than a wholesale commitment to stop living for self and to start living for God. Repentance takes us to the heart of worship.

In the first chapter of his letter to the Roman church, St Paul speaks of a deadly exchange. He tells the story of how mankind in its foolishness did not honour God even though God's presence has been made evident to us. *'Claiming to be wise, they became fools; and they exchanged the glory of the immortal God for images resembling a mortal human being or birds or four-footed animals or reptiles.' (Romans 1:22-23, NRSV)* He explains how we have willingly chosen to give the glory that belongs to God to that which is less than God. What we have done is traded in a relationship with the God of heaven for a life of self-seeking, and robbed God of the glory and honour that belongs to Him as supremely desirable, such that we can give our devotion to the things of this world. This is nothing less than exchanging life for death.

In Jeremiah 2:13, God speaks to us through the prophet: *'my people have committed two evils: they have forsaken me, the fountain of living water, and dug out cisterns for themselves, cracked cisterns that can hold no water.' (NRSV)* In this statement we see the foolishness of the exchange. At best the false gods of this age and all the things we might be tempted to place our confidence in are no better than cracked cisterns that promise refreshment but deliver disappointment, for they cannot satisfy the deepest longings of the soul. Ultimately, they prove empty consolation. God, on the other hand, is a fountain of living water, a stream that never runs dry.

In his encounter with the woman at the well in John chapter 4, Jesus develops this theme. In the heat of the noon-day sun, Jesus sits down by a well just as a Samaritan woman approaches to draw water. Jesus engages the woman in a rather cryptic dialogue about water, asking her for a drink and using the presence of the well to open up a conversation about spiritual refreshment: *Jesus said to her, 'Everyone who drinks of this water will be thirsty again, but those who drink of the water that I will give them will never be thirsty. The water that I will give will become in them a spring of water gushing up to eternal life.' (John 4:13-14, NRSV)* Jesus gently and humbly invites us to consider the difference between the empty promises of sin and the truly life-giving nature of God. The things of this world can never truly satisfy the soul that is made for the things of heaven.

As the conversation unfolds, Jesus reveals some sensitive details about the woman's love life, and she quickly changes the subject by raising a contentious question about where God is to be worshipped. Jesus is drawing the woman's attention to the hunger in her own soul, a hunger that has no doubt been manifesting through a series of broken relationships, but has not found any fulfilment in them. Indeed, the deepest yearnings of the human soul can only be satisfied in Jesus and true worship is less a matter of physical geography as it is a matter of recognising God Himself to be the one in whom our souls find their rest. Those who worship God must do so *'in spirit and in truth' (John 4:23, NRSV).*

When we repent, we are recognising that our own efforts to live without God have left us dry and thirsty. When we repent, we are first of all making a break with the idolatries with which we reject God either knowingly or unknowingly and we recommit ourselves to true worship.

Worship is not simply one aspect of Christian living; worship is the fullest expression of our humanity. Worship is humanity in right relationship with God. When we seek to do all things for love of Christ and in accordance with His will, including things we might be tempted to think of as secular, the whole of our lives become a solemn offering of worship to God. Worship is no longer something we do, but something we become. We are to be worshipping people, not just in church but wherever we might find ourselves, and true worship takes place in the heart.

During worship our eyes are raised to heaven. When we pray or sing hymns with attention and affection, or whenever we participate in the sacramental life of the Church, we also renew our vision. St Paul admonishes us in this regard: *'Let the word of Christ dwell in you richly; teach and admonish one another in all wisdom; and with gratitude in your hearts sing psalms, hymns, and spiritual songs to God. And whatever you do, in word or deed, do everything in the name of the Lord Jesus, giving thanks to God the Father through him.' (Colossians 3:16-17, NRSV)* Praise and gratitude are to fill our hearts such that the whole shape of our lives is reformed for His glory.

Regular worship is vital for a life of true repentance because not only is it essential for nurturing intimacy with the God of heaven, but it changes the way we see and it helps us to view the whole of our lives with all of our problems and issues in the light of God's glory. So often our issues and our fears stem from a view of God that is far too small. If anything, there can never be a vision of God that is too big. Even with an eternity in His presence we could never exhaust the depths of His being and the riches of his grace. Our sins and our problems might seem overwhelming. From the perspective of earth, they might loom large over us, engulfing us in their shadow. This can be a frightening and discouraging experience. It is easy to become despondent and to believe the lie that there is nothing to be done.

All the while as we focus on the problems of our sins and the dilemmas we face, they seem to grow larger in our minds and the memory of God can fade, such that we begin to lose faith in Him. We end up with a distorted picture, consisting of a huge problem and a small and distant God, not adequate to save us. Worship and time spent contemplating God's glory works to correct our perspective. Time spent in adoration and contemplation of God renews our sense of God as almighty and all-compassionate. As our vision of God grows, increasing exponentially as we come closer to Him and become more familiar with Him, so the barriers that seemed so insurmountable are seen as increasingly small beside Him. Yes, to us our issues might seem overwhelming, but nothing is too big for the power of God and no sin is too dirty to be cleansed by the blood of Jesus. Whenever we are tempted to give in or run in fear, then we should worship and renew our vision of God.

> *I pray that the God of our Lord Jesus Christ, the Father of glory, may give you a spirit of wisdom and revelation as you come to know him, so that, with the eyes of your heart enlightened,*

you may know what is the hope to which he has called you, what are the riches of his glorious inheritance among the saints, and what is the immeasurable greatness of his power for us who believe, according to the working of his great power. (Ephesians 1:17-19, NRSV)

St Paul prays that his children in Ephesus would have such a renewed vision, knowing that such knowledge of God is itself only possible by the workings of God's Spirit. All that we can ever truly know of God comes by the light of the Holy Spirit who leads us into truth. *'For with you is the fountain of life; in your light we see light.' (Psalm 36:9, NRSV)* In worship we cast the light of God's presence upon the shadows of our sins and we see how great is His mercy and how powerful is His hand to save and deliver. We slowly learn to stop looking at the things of heaven from earth's perspective and instead to regard the things of this world from heaven's perspective, where God has *'seated us with him in the heavenly places in Christ Jesus' (Ephesians 2:6, NRSV).* Worship corrects both our vision and our perspective.

As we read through the New Testament, we find time after time the instruction to cultivate a heart of gratitude, which is perhaps the only appropriate response to the revelation of God's loving kindness towards us. Cultivating gratitude helps us to remember that we live by the grace of God and that all that we have is the fruit of His love and His ongoing care. Gratitude fosters humility because it turns the attention away from ourselves and towards God, which is exactly the movement of the penitent heart. Further, we are encouraged to give thanks in every circumstance, the good, the bad and the ugly. We are called to praise God for His goodness, even when it seems like everything has gone pear-shaped, and to see in our moments of trial opportunities to deepen our trust in God and to lean more fully on Him.

In the incredibly joy-filled letter of Philippians, St Paul writes: *'Do not worry about anything, but in everything by prayer and supplication with thanksgiving let your requests be made known to God. And the peace of God, which surpasses all understanding, will guard your hearts and your minds in Christ Jesus.' (Philippians 4:6-7, NRSV)* Thanksgiving in the face of adversity is a profound act of trust in the goodness of God, it truly honours Him. It took a while for me to get to grips with this verse, but one day about five years ago I was praying alone in church. I had some music on and I was singing 'Holy, holy, holy', simply delighting in singing my praises to God. As I turned to scripture, this passage from Philippians 4 came to my attention and so I tucked the verse away in my heart. Later that day, my wife and I were going for the twelve-week scan for our second child and we were excited.

I can remember sitting in the waiting room with our oldest child, nervously anticipating the re-emergence of my wife from the scanning room. Eventually a nurse came out and called me through. I knew something was wrong. The nurse led me into the room where my wife was waiting and I discovered that our little baby was poorly. Over the next few weeks, we found out that he had Edward's Syndrome and that due to serious physical and mental handicaps our little child probably would not make it. The strange thing was that at that moment, I could not get the song 'holy, holy, holy' out of my head, and St Paul's exhortation to give thanks in everything, kept popping into my mind. In that moment I decided to test the promise. Quietly in my heart I thanked God for his goodness and praised him. What followed was a deep sense of peace, a peace I still cannot quite understand, a sense of being held, like a little boat held up by the vast ocean beneath. I still felt the pain, I still cried, and I still suffered the agony of the weeks that followed. But in all of it I knew that God was at work and I knew that I was loved and held by Him. Christ truly guarded my heart and mind. Thanksgiving and worship are a truly powerful thing, protecting our minds from the enemy who would use our trials to devour our faith.

'Humble yourselves therefore under the mighty hand of God, so that he may exalt you in due time. Cast all your anxiety on him, because he cares for you. Discipline yourselves; keep alert. Like a roaring lion your

adversary the devil prowls around, looking for someone to devour.' (1 Peter 5:6-8, NRSV)

As we stand in the light of God's presence and live with thanksgiving in our hearts for the mercies of God and for His immeasurable goodness towards us who have sinned against Him, our hearts are moved to deeper repentance. This time, instead of repentance that flows from fear of punishment or fear of missing out on eternity with God, we begin to taste of the fear that is born of love. As our hearts grow in thanksgiving and our repentance deepens, our desire for purity and for holiness is stirred up by the fear that we might offend God whom we love so dearly. It is the fear of scorning His love and trampling on His blood that helps us to pursue godliness. As our desire to be with God grows, as we taste the sweetness of communion, so we come to abhor everything within us that threatens to come between us and our beloved; we fear losing him. As King David cried out, *'Create in me a clean heart, O God, and put a new and right spirit within me. Do not cast me away from your presence, and do not take your holy spirit from me.' (Psalm 51:10-11, NRSV)* But again, we recognise that unless God acts within us, creating within us clean hearts, we are helpless. Therefore, our cries for mercy become stronger and the closer we come to God in His awesome holiness the more clearly we see both our own sin and God's grace. Together this dual knowledge presses our repentance deeper; we know how much we need God, but we also know how much He delights to help His children.

Similarly, when we see our own sins against God's love in the light of God's mercy towards us, then the thought of His kindness again gives energy to our repentance. *'Do you despise the riches of his kindness and forbearance and patience? Do you not realize that God's kindness is meant to lead you to repentance?' (Romans 2:4, NRSV)* Worship and thanksgiving in this sense become both a fruit and a cause of repentance.

Whenever I look at a source of light such as a window or the rays of the sun piercing through the foliage of the summer trees, I often like to close to my eyes and see how the shapes created by the light remain imprinted on my vision, even with my eyes closed. There is a kind of memory formed in the eye that increases in strength the brighter the source of light becomes. In worship, as we gaze on the beauty of God, the vision of His goodness leaves a kind of imprint on us, and our calling is to be so filled with the thought of God that even in the darkness we still perceive His light.

Repentance is in part the cultivating of the memory of God. Through the fall, our inner life has become divided and fragmented. We were created with a simple inner unity, heart and mind united, such that like the cherubim in Ezekiel's vision we might simply move instinctively as God wills, and in this movement find our deepest joy. *'Each moved straight ahead; wherever the spirit would go, they went, without turning as they went.' (Ezekiel 1:12, NRSV)* But through sin and the effects of the fall, we have splintered our inner life and we find that we now have to deliberate over what the best course of action might be, or else we find ourselves in 'two minds' over something. In such a state, with so many thoughts and anxieties swirling around, it can be hard to hold on to the simple memory of God as we were created to do. Through repentance our inner life is slowly healed and, by God's grace, our essential inner unity is restored, such that our will is increasingly conformed to God's will and our hearts become naturally more sensitive and responsive to God's call. In worship, we seek with attention and love and with God's help to pull together our dispersed faculties and to bring the whole of ourselves, body, mind, heart and soul, before God in a movement of love, making of the triune God our singular focus and our stable centre.

Chapter 13

A Transformed Life

Having spent so much time thinking about what repentance could look like in our daily living it might be tempting to imagine that repentance is the chief end of the Christian life. Repentance, however, is not so much an end in itself, as it is the means through which we enter into a greater joy, a more human life, a life that does justice to the intentions of God in creating us. Repentance opens us up to the saving life of Christ to whom we are united in the power of Holy Spirit. Our ultimate end is supposed to be union with God. Questions about repentance are necessarily bound up with questions about our salvation and even our salvation is not an end in itself, but the means by which God might be glorified in his saints and in his Church (Ephesians 3:20-21). St Paul states numerous times in Ephesians, for example, that God's great movement of love for the sake of the salvation of humanity is ultimately for the praise of his glorious grace. Indeed, God's glory is seen in his mercy and compassion: *Moses said, 'Show me your glory, I pray.' And he said, 'I will make all my goodness pass before you, and will proclaim before you the name,*

"The Lord"; and I will be gracious to whom I will be gracious, and will show mercy on whom I will show mercy. (Exodus 33:18-19, NRSV) God is glorified in showing himself strong against sin and death, and God is glorified in the lives of the saints who increasingly come to shine with His light: *'Let your light shine before others, so that they may see your good works and give glory to your Father in heaven' (Matthew 5:16, NRSV)*.

One of the most beautiful and striking scenes in the gospels is the transfiguration of Christ (Matthew 17:1-8; Mark 9:2-8; Luke 9:28-36). Whilst on his way to Jerusalem where He would soon be crucified, Jesus took Peter, James and John up a mountain to pray. As He prayed Jesus was transfigured before them, both His clothes and His flesh shone with a dazzling light, which the evangelist Mark says were whiter than any human could bleach them, so pure and radiant was His presence. Indeed, only God can make the things of this world, including our humanity, as spotless as Christ appeared that day. Then, as this was happening, Moses and Elijah appeared beside Him and began to speak with Him about His departure, His own Exodus. They spoke about the death and resurrection through which He would lead His people to freedom from sin, just as Moses had led the Israelites through the Red sea from slavery into freedom. Peter wanted to prolong the occasion and offered to build shelters for Jesus and the two holy men beside Him, but suddenly a great cloud appeared, the cloud of God's manifest presence, and from the cloud the voice of God spoke, saying *'This is my Son, the Beloved; with him I am well pleased; listen to him!' (Matthew 17:6, NRSV).* In that moment Christ was revealed to the disciples as He really is. It is not so much that He changed in that moment, but rather that the eyes of the three apostles were opened to see Christ as He has always been. In Christ, the humanity of Jesus is completely united to and transformed by His divinity. Jesus is God made flesh and, as the very Son of God incarnate, we should listen to Him.

This event takes place on the way to Jerusalem, where Jesus will soon die. After His transfiguration, Jesus takes the time to remind His disciples that He will be betrayed, suffer and die at the hands of men. The glory of God revealed on the mountain that day shines out amidst the shadow of His impending crucifixion. We are supposed to understand, I think, that the way to glory is through the cross, and that the glory and majesty of God are seen most clearly in His sacrificial death and the resurrection that follows. So too our own transformation must come through a participation in the death and resurrection of Jesus; the death of repentance must precede our renewal in the Spirit.

In this scene, although Jesus is revealed as He is and always shall be, we also catch a glimpse of what we are to become in Him and by the power of His

Spirit. Jesus reveals to us the reality of human nature untied to and filled with the very life of God; always human, but nevertheless transformed into His likeness. This is our calling and this is the end of our salvation, to be united to Christ in a life like His. As the apostle John was to later write: *'Beloved, we are God's children now; what we will be has not yet been revealed. What we do know is this: when he is revealed, we will be like him, for we will see him as he is. And all who have this hope in him purify themselves, just as he is pure.' (1 John 3:2-3, NRSV)* As those who live in the hope of future transformation and a sharing in Christ's divine life, we should take seriously the call to purity, to holiness.

In the Sermon on the Mount Jesus calls us to *'Be perfect, therefore, as your heavenly Father is perfect.' (Matthew 5:48, NRSV)* Later, the apostle Peter, who also witnessed the transfiguration, states that *'as he who called you is holy, be holy yourselves in all your conduct; for it is written, 'You shall be holy, for I am holy.' (1 Peter 1:15-16, NRSV)* Our call is a call to perfection and to holiness. Our salvation is more than a change of legal status before God. When the Scriptures speak of our justification, it would be to diminish the fulness of Christ's sacrificial death and resurrection to say that all we get is a 'not guilty' verdict instead of a 'guilty' one. If all that changes is that someone else has taken our punishment so that we can be spared it, then we are still sinners in our nature and nothing has really changed, we are just sinners let off the hook. But St Paul is clear: *'if anyone is in Christ, there is a new creation: everything old has passed away; see, everything has become new!'* (2 Corinthians 5:15, NRSV). Certainly, Jesus forgives us our sins and his crucifixion pays their debt, removing the legal demands against us, but something deeper is happening here too. In order to draw close to God our very nature needs to be renewed. We need to actually *be* holy and to actually *be* perfect in order to draw close to God; a real transformation needs to happen.

Whenever someone is united to Christ in His death and resurrection through faith in Him and by His glorious grace, then not only are sins forgiven, but a renewal of the whole person begins. This process of renewal begins at the moment of baptism and, if we embrace it through continued openness and responsiveness to the Spirit's work in our lives, then it continues throughout our earthly life and on into eternity. *'Now the Lord is the Spirit, and where the Spirit of the Lord is, there is freedom. And all of us, with unveiled faces, seeing the glory of the Lord as though reflected in a mirror, are being transformed into the same image from one degree of glory to another; for this comes from the Lord, the Spirit.' (2 Corinthians 3:17-18, NRSV)* Transformation evermore into the likeness of Christ comes by the Spirit who makes us free and is at the very heart of our calling. We cooperate with the Spirit by repentance. The Spirit of

God alone works this great sanctifying work in us, but He will not force it on those who neither desire it nor seek it.

As we reflect on our calling, it becomes clear that repentance really does lead to joy. What could be more joyful than to be so close to God that we are transformed into His likeness? What could be more joyful than to increasingly learn to walk in the freedom of the Spirit, whose presence is life? Christian history offers us numerous testimonies of the saints who through profound faith and deep repentance literally began to shine with the light of Christ, their very bodies radiant with the joy of His Kingdom. Such lives not only release the aroma of Christ, but also draw many to the Saviour in whom they too might find their freedom. Freedom from sin is only half the story. If that were all that we needed, then the death of Jesus would have been enough. What completes our salvation is renewal in the Spirit, made possible by the power of the resurrection. We are set free from sin and in that moment released for a life of willing service to God, such that we might be united to Him and become like Him. Freedom from sin, and freedom to live. Death and resurrection. Atonement and transformation. Justification and sanctification. In repentance we turn our backs on sin, lay hold of the atoning work of Christ and commit ourselves to the Spirit's work of renewal in our hearts.

Conclusion

Onwards into Joy

The invitation of Jesus is an invitation into life. Jesus calls us to surrender everything to Him and promises that this is the very means by which we lay hold of the life that He gives. At the Eucharist the assembly of God's people presents a simple offering of bread and wine. Both the wine and the bread cannot be made unless first their basic ingredients are crushed. These elements remind us of the Lord's command for those who follow Him to come and die. So too do they remind us of the crushing by which He gives us life. The gifts are then taken into the priest's hands and he gives thanks over them. The simplicity of these humble gifts represents the ordinariness of our lives, lives that might seem small and meagre to us, but which are incredibly precious to God. As the priest takes and blesses the bread and the wine, they are transformed, filled mystically with the very life of God. The bread becomes Christ's body in a manner beyond our understanding and the wine becomes His blood. These humble gifts are elevated by the indwelling presence of Christ and returned to us for our life and salvation. Christ comes to us in bread and wine such that we might feast on Him and live.

'Very truly, I tell you, unless you eat the flesh of the Son of Man and drink his blood, you have no life in you. Those who eat my flesh and drink my blood have eternal life, and I will raise them up on the last day; for my flesh is true food and my blood is true drink. Those who eat my flesh and drink my blood abide in me, and I in them.'
(John 6:53-56, NRSV)

The action of the Eucharist in many ways reflects the basic movement of our faith. In trusting surrender, we place everything that we are and all that we have into Christ's hands. He then takes our offering and returns it to us, this time transformed by His life and filled with His presence. What we receive far surpasses all that we give. It is a treasure for which we must not be afraid to let everything else go. When Christ calls us to die, His intention for us is abundant life, a life we cannot receive unless we first let go of this one. In repentance we recognise that in grasping after the comforts and pleasures of this earthly life we actually hasten our death. In repentance we recognise that in humbling ourselves before God, seeking to be crucified with Him, we enter into His very own life.

There is much more that could be said in a little book like this and there is much more that I still have to learn myself. But my hope is that, in reading this book, you have been encouraged to pursue Christ with greater devotion and more ardent love. Repentance is a lifetime's work and there are always times when we might be tempted to give up, just as surely as there are days when our closeness to God opens up new depths of joy in Him. I encourage you to keep going, to resolve every day to walk further the way of the cross. God's heart rejoices whenever we turn back to Him in faith. He loves us and His promise for those who turn to Him is everlasting life. As St Peter proclaims:

> *Repent therefore, and turn to God so that your sins may be wiped out, so that times of refreshing may come from the presence of the Lord. (Acts 3:19-20, NRSV)*

Times of refreshing - that is what we need. Refreshment comes from the presence of the Lord and our repentance is about nothing less than being with Him whom we love. But all of this is a work of God's grace, and so, as we recommit to lives of heartfelt penitence, let us also pray for one another, that each of us together might shine to the glory of God the Father.

Lord Jesus Christ, Son of God, have mercy upon us.

Lightning Source UK Ltd.
Milton Keynes UK
UKHW041833211020
371977UK00003B/953